# Elegant Inks

## Make your own greeting cards and frameable art using crayons, markers, or colored pencils on beautiful pen and ink drawings created by Louise Jackson M.D.A.

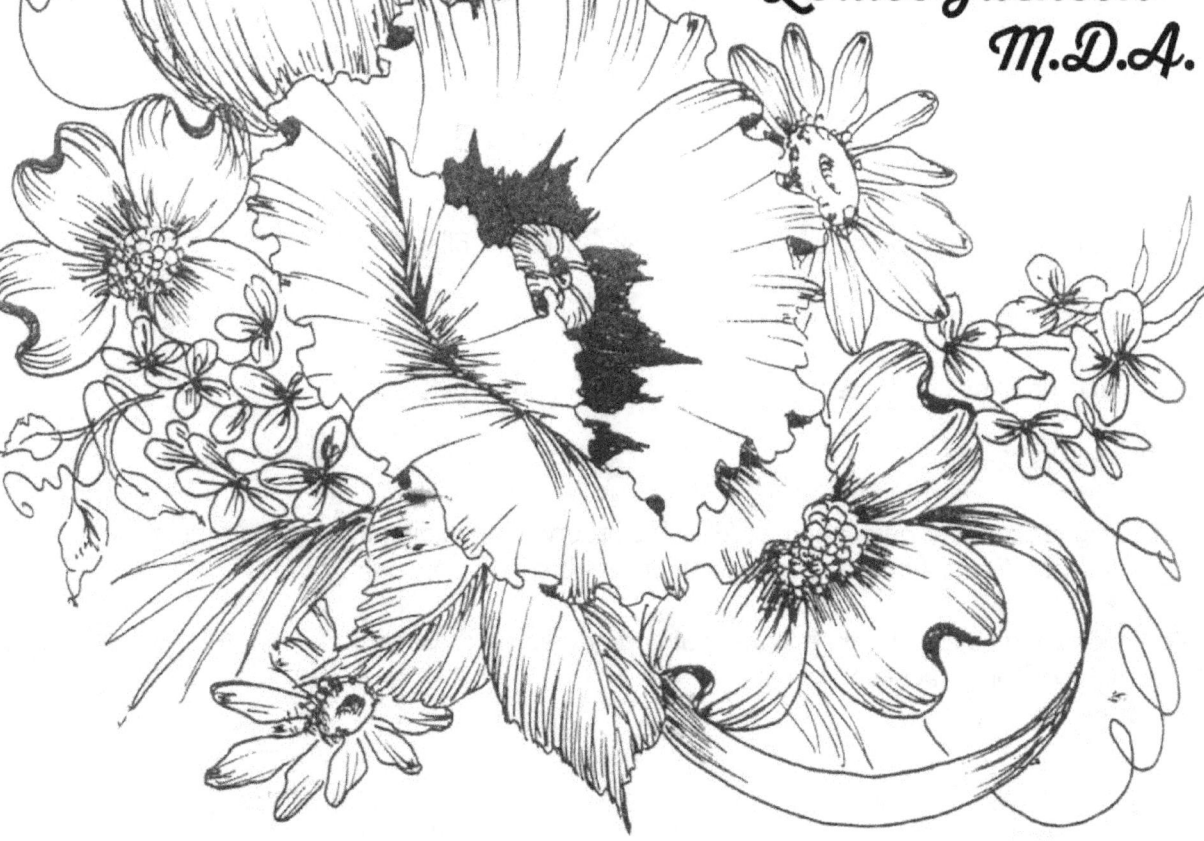

Elegant Inks is an original publication by Garden Creek Gallery Publishing

Copyright © 2017 by Louise Jackson

Images and Drawings © by Louise Jackson

ISBN-13: 978-1543157215

## ABOUT THE ARTIST

Louise Jackson has been a multimedia artist who works in oils, acrylics, watercolor and inks since 1965. She's the author of 23 painting tutorial books, has been featured in and on the cover of dozens of magazines, has appeared on television and been featured in videos teaching portrait, floral, abstract, and still life paintings.

She is a member of the Dayton Society of Painters and Sculptors, Western Ohio Watercolor Society, and is a Master Decorative Artist with the Society of Decorative Painters. Her work is on display at the Smithsonian and the Decorative Arts Collection Museum in Atlanta, Georgia in addition to many private and corporate collections.

Louise loves sharing her joy of painting with students around the world. She has taught in Italy, Japan, Canada, Argentina, and all over the United States including Hawaii.

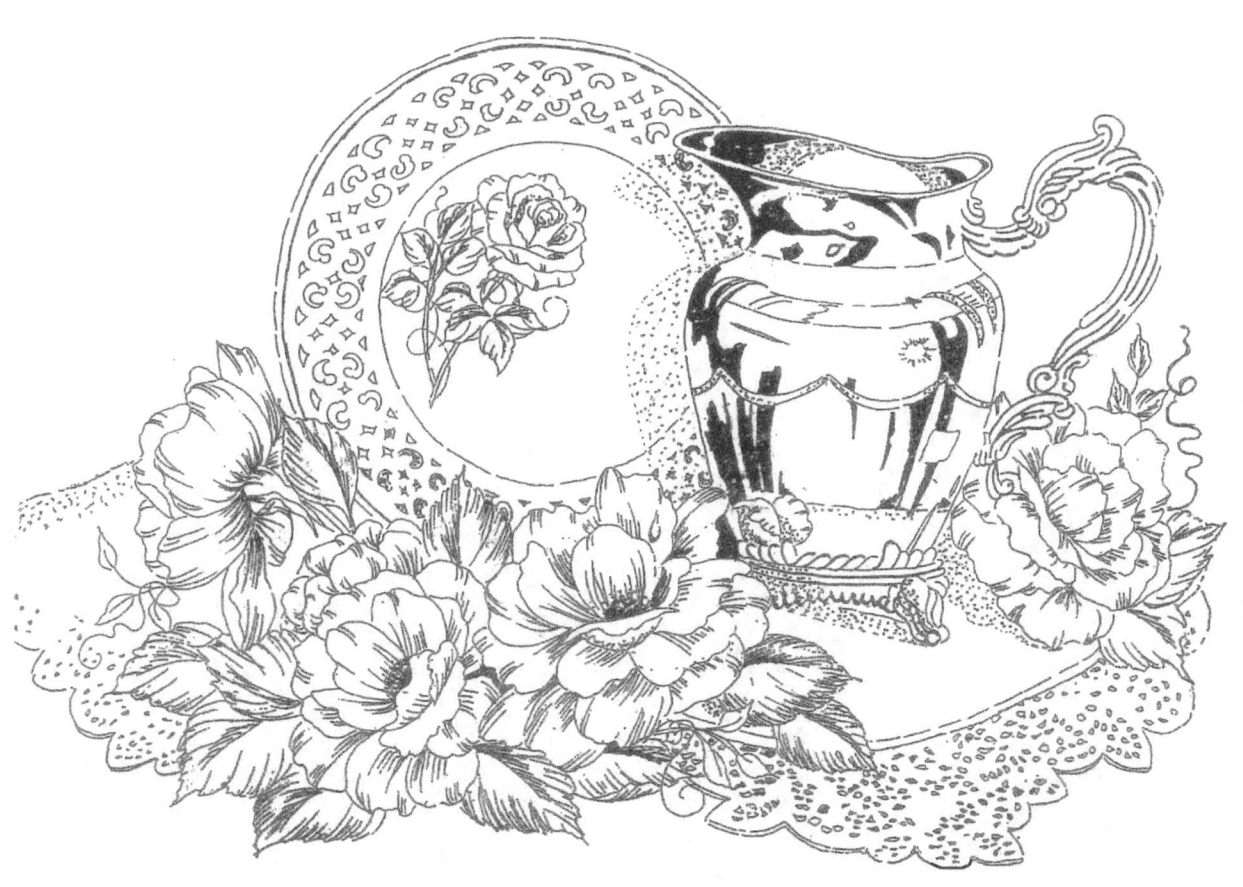

Enjoy coloring your own greeting cards and frameable art using
crayons, colored markers or colored pencils.
To create a greeting card carefully cut the card pages out of
the coloring book, fold in half, sign and add a special note.

The full size coloring pages can be removed and placed in a mat and frame
or simply hung on your refrigerator.

If you'd like to use paint to color these inked designs,
transfer the drawings onto watercolor paper by
placing a piece of graphite paper between the coloring page and the
watercolor paper and tracing over the lines in the drawing.

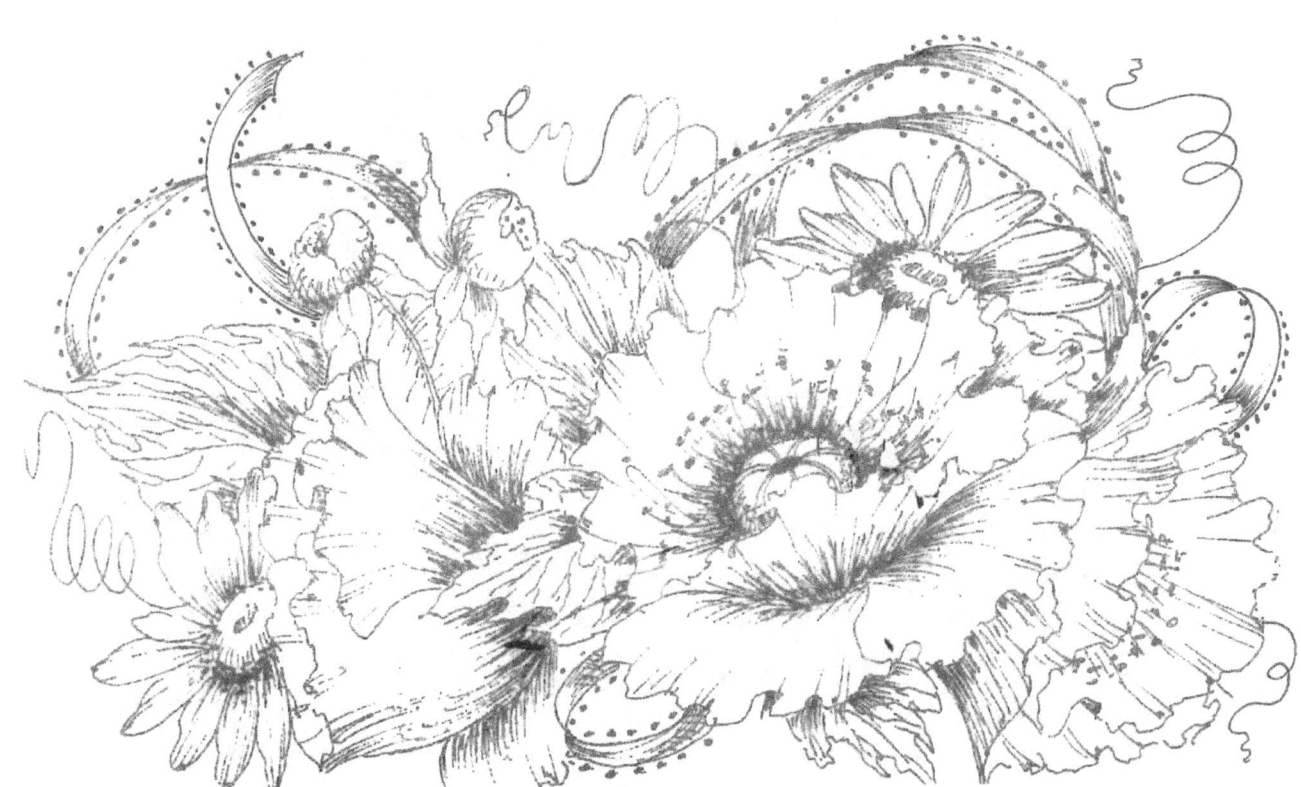

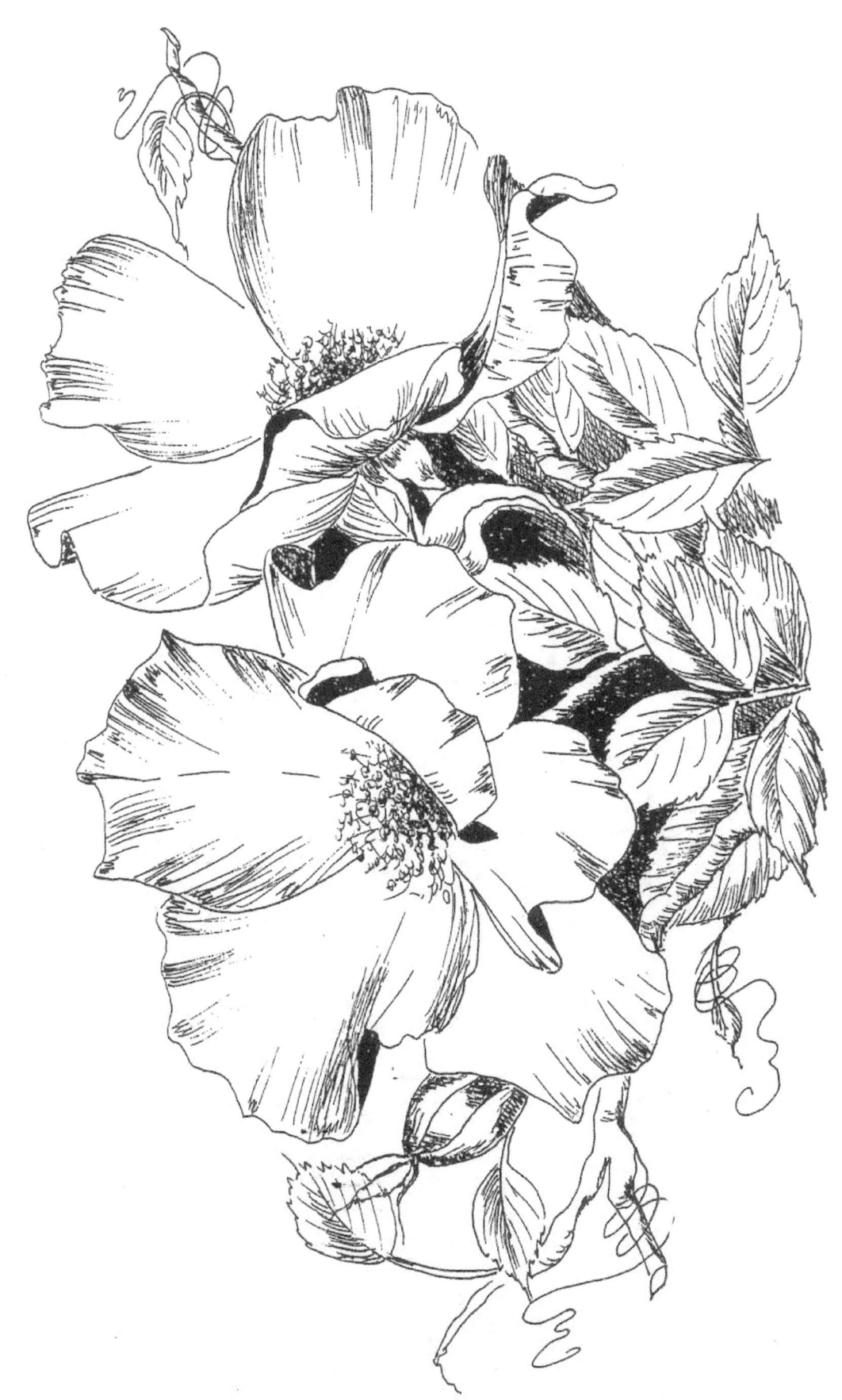

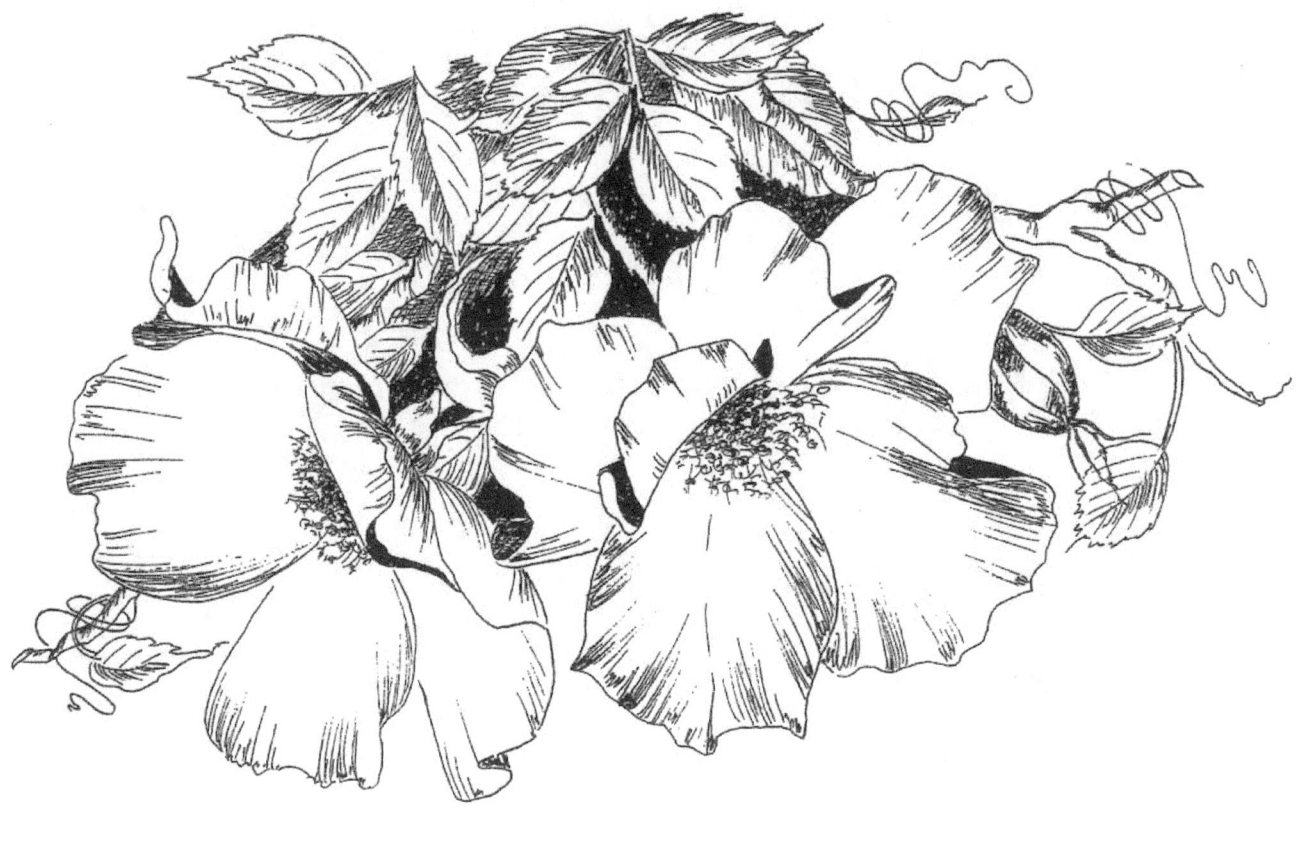

This card has been designed

with care and love especially

for you. It is suitable for framing.

Original drawing by

Louise Jackson, M.D.A.

Artistically colored by

_____

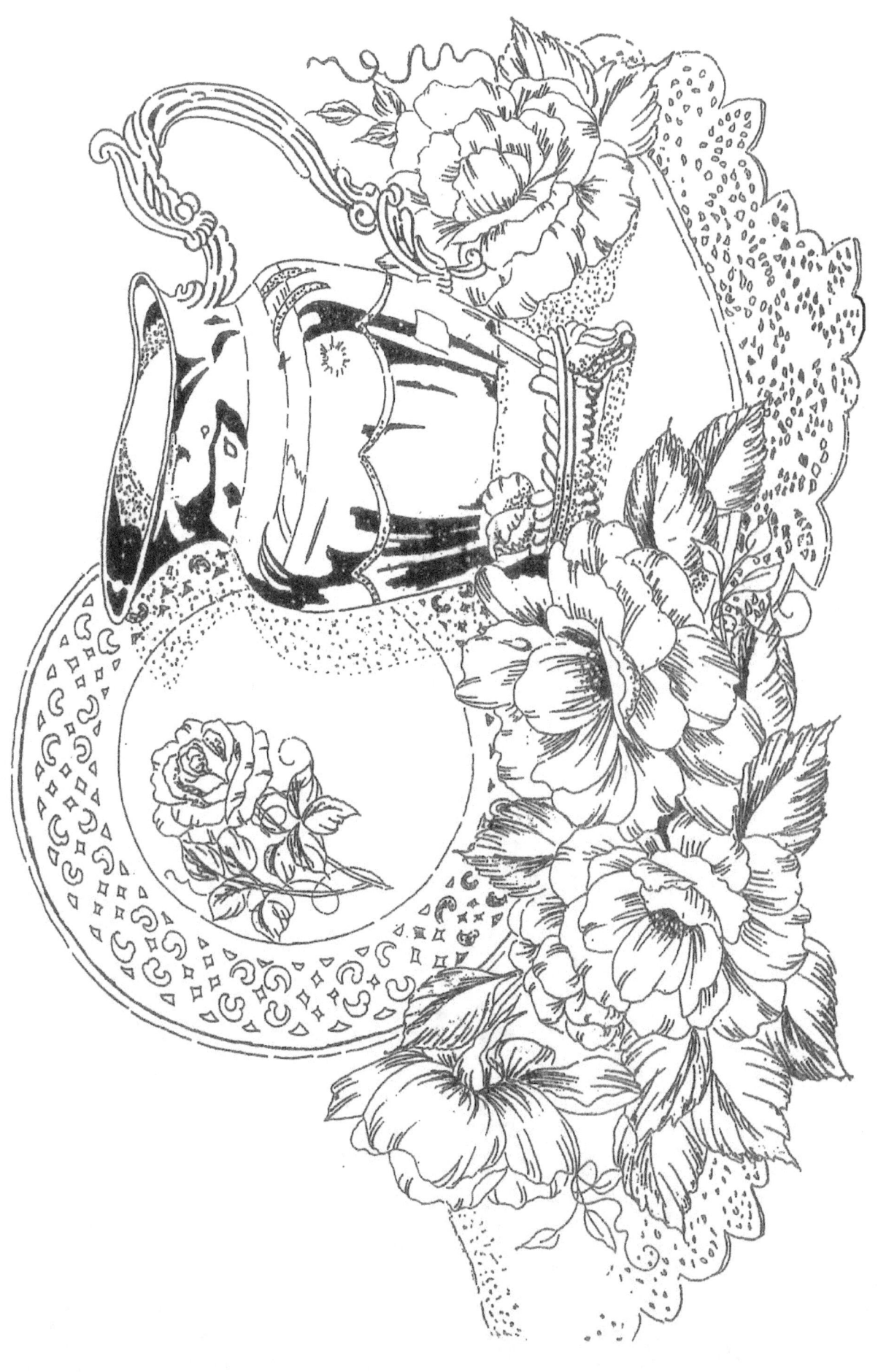

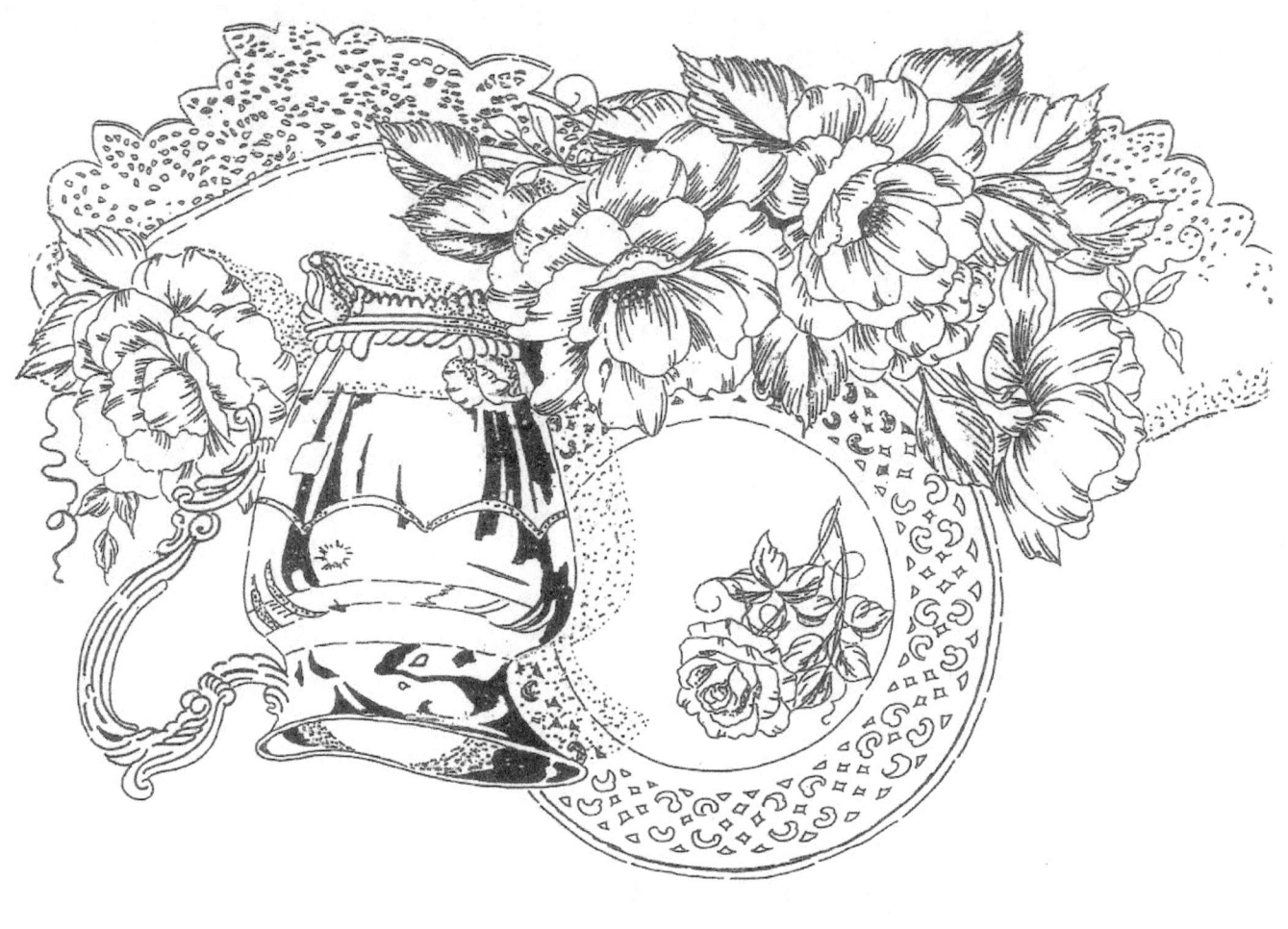

This card has been designed

with care and love especially

for you. It is suitable for framing.

Original drawing by

Louise Jackson, M.D.A.

Artistically colored by

_____

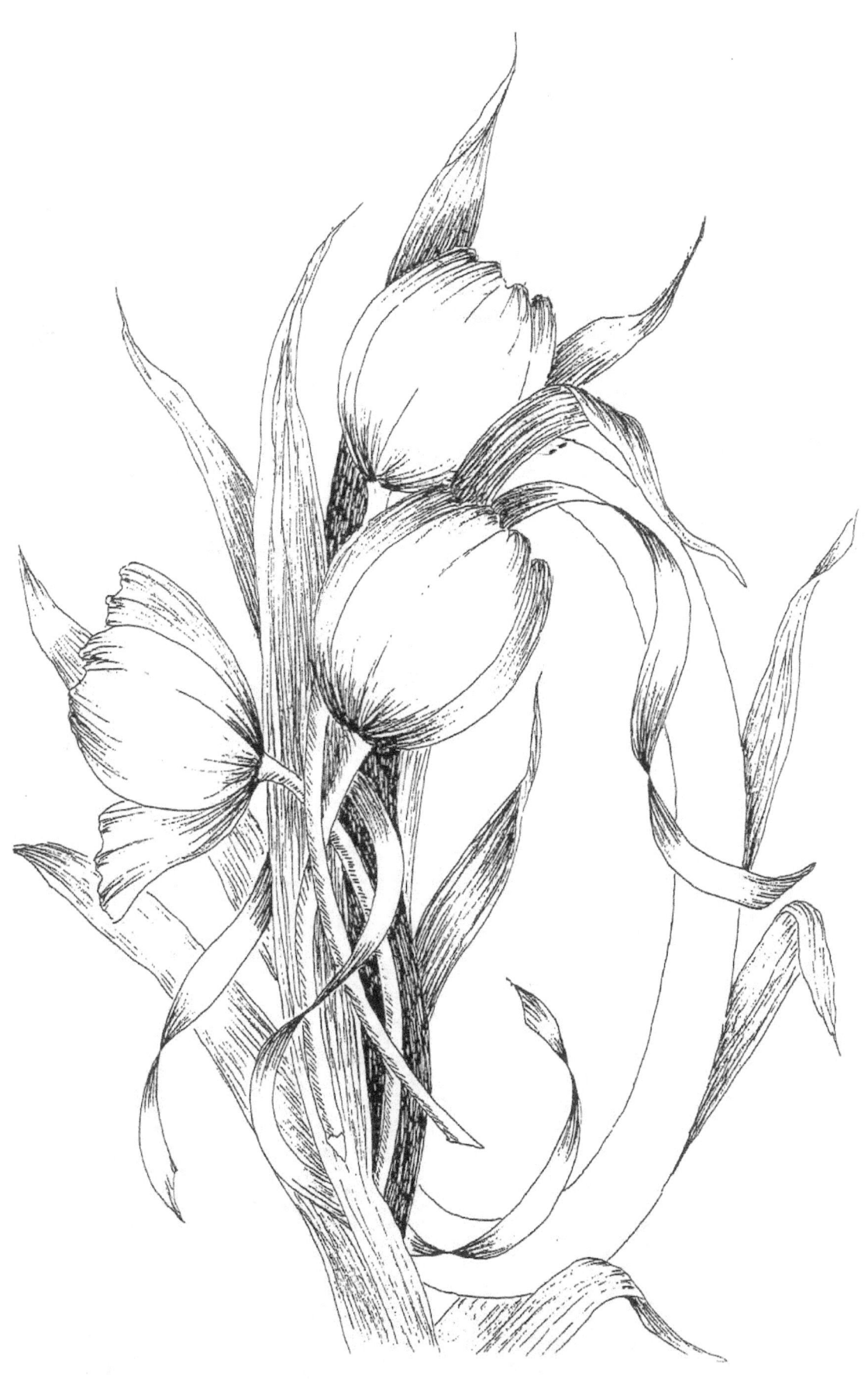

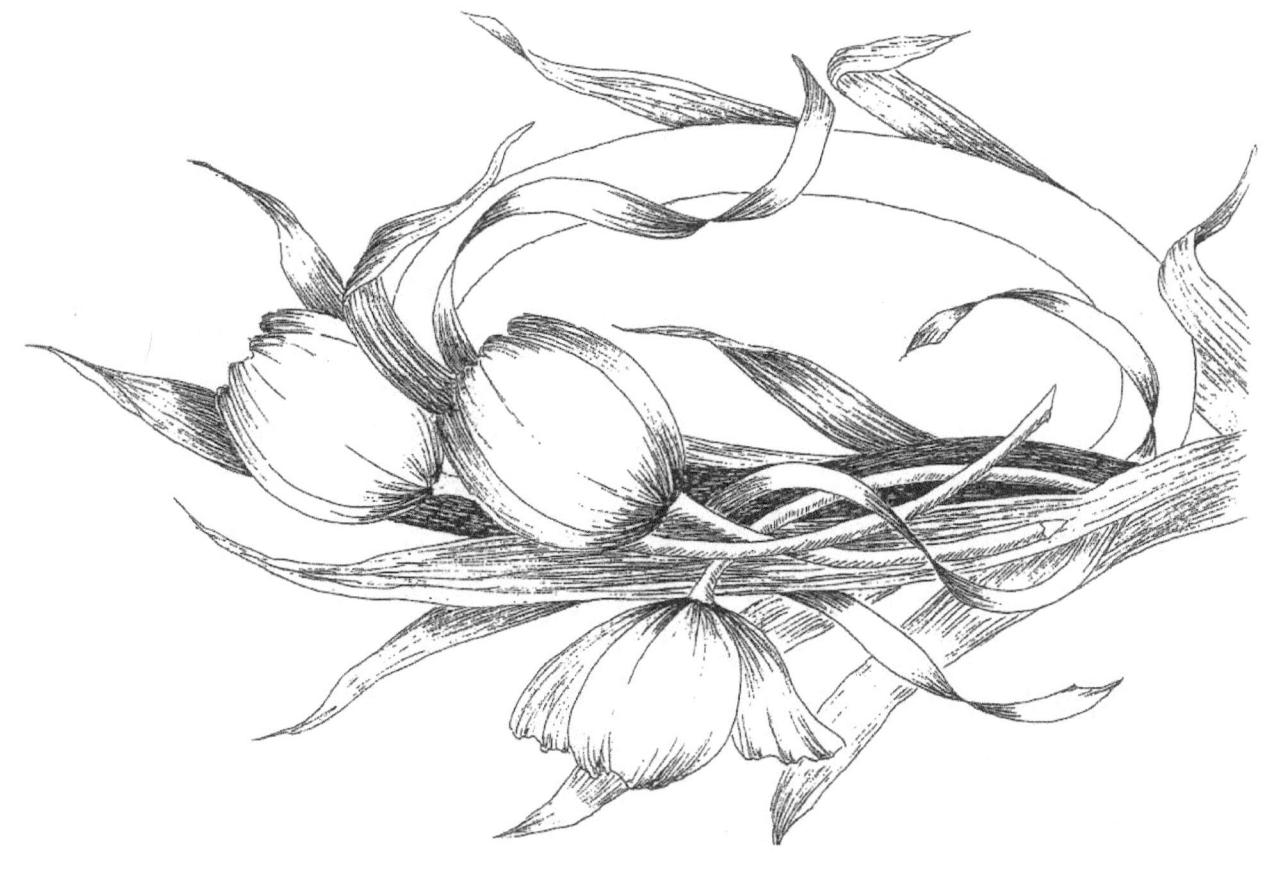

This card has been designed

with care and love especially

for you. It is suitable for framing.

Original drawing by

Louise Jackson, M.D.A.

Artistically colored by

_____

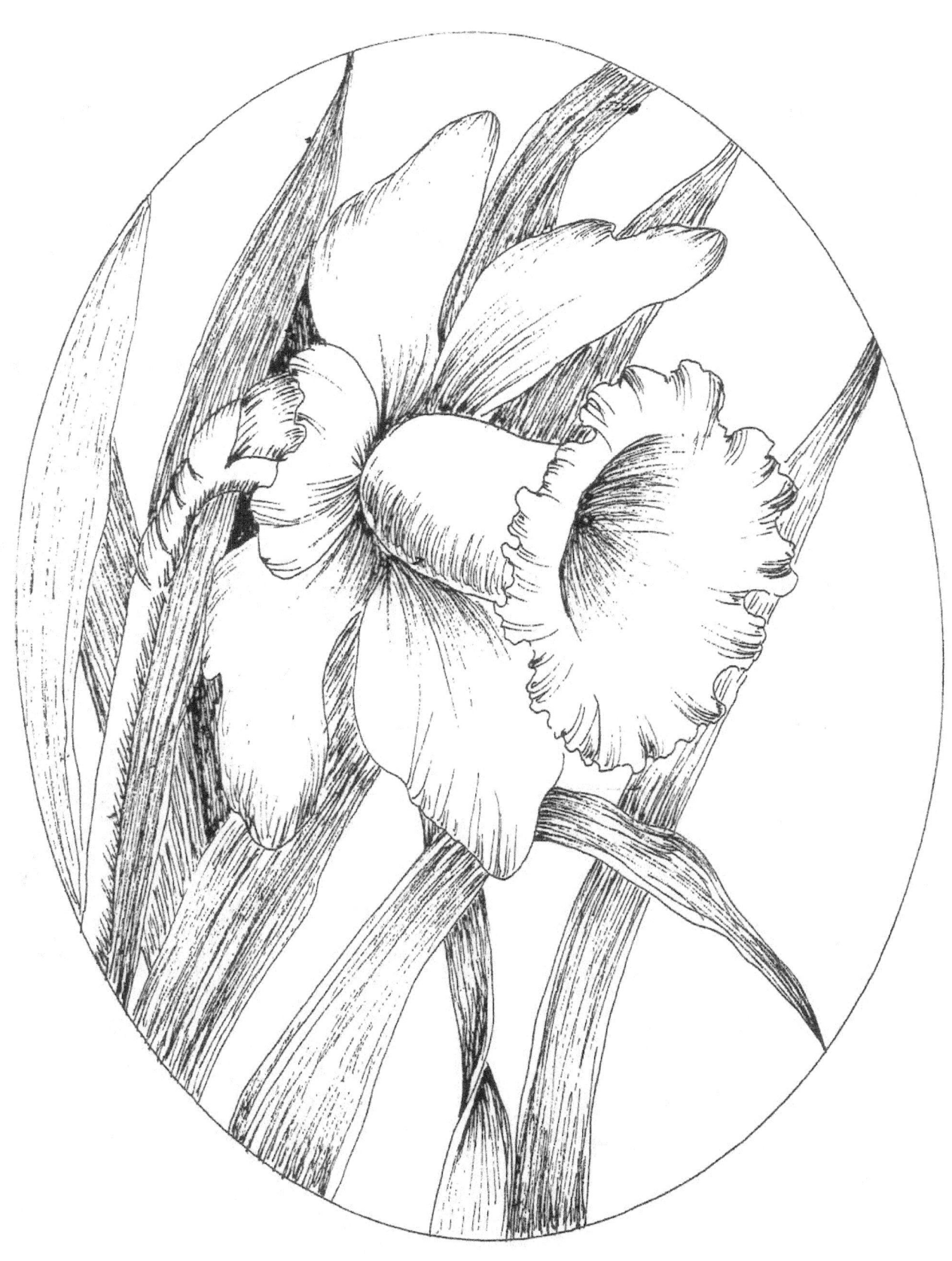

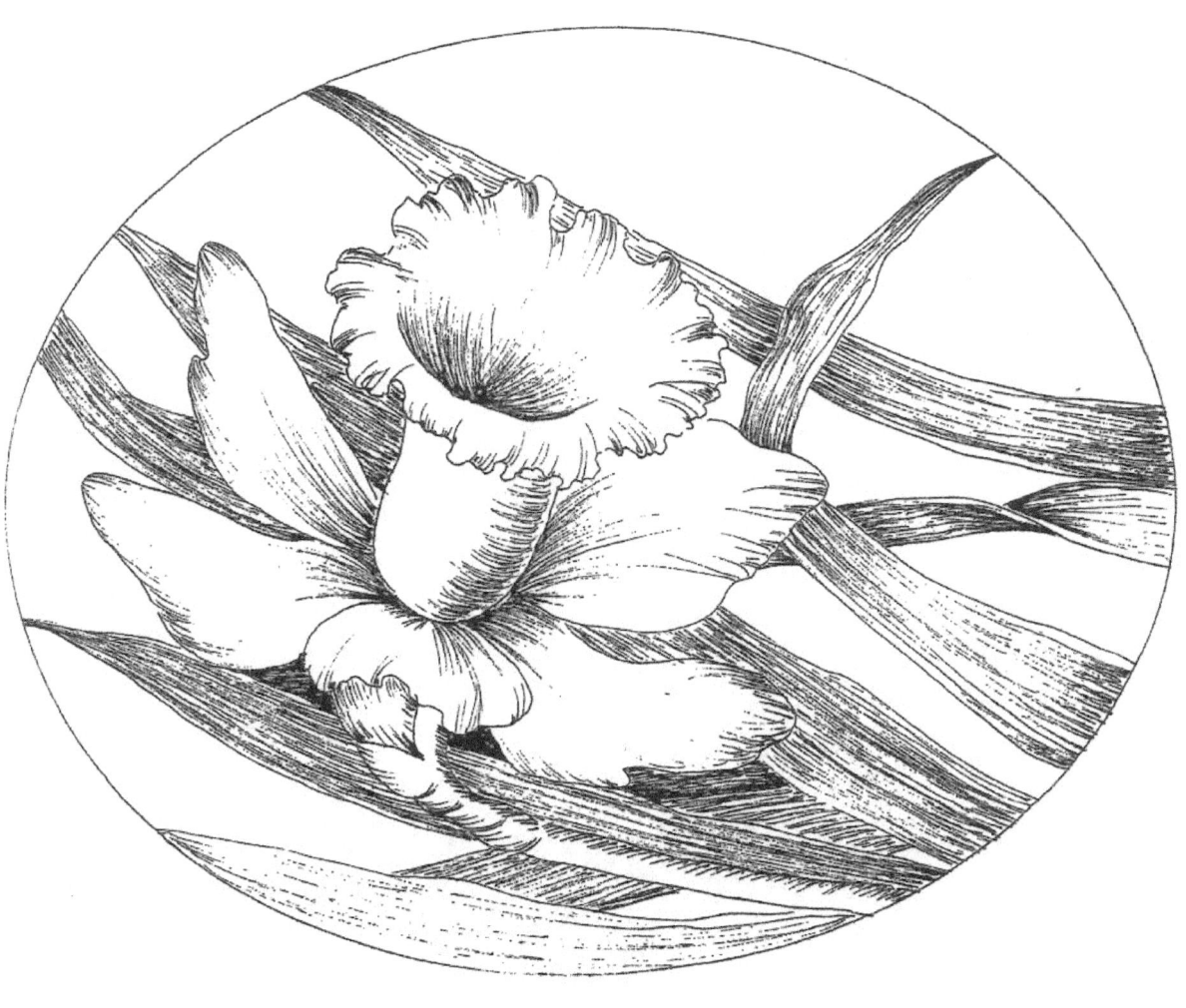

This card has been designed

with care and love especially

for you. It is suitable for framing.

Original drawing by

Louise Jackson, M.D.A.

Artistically colored by

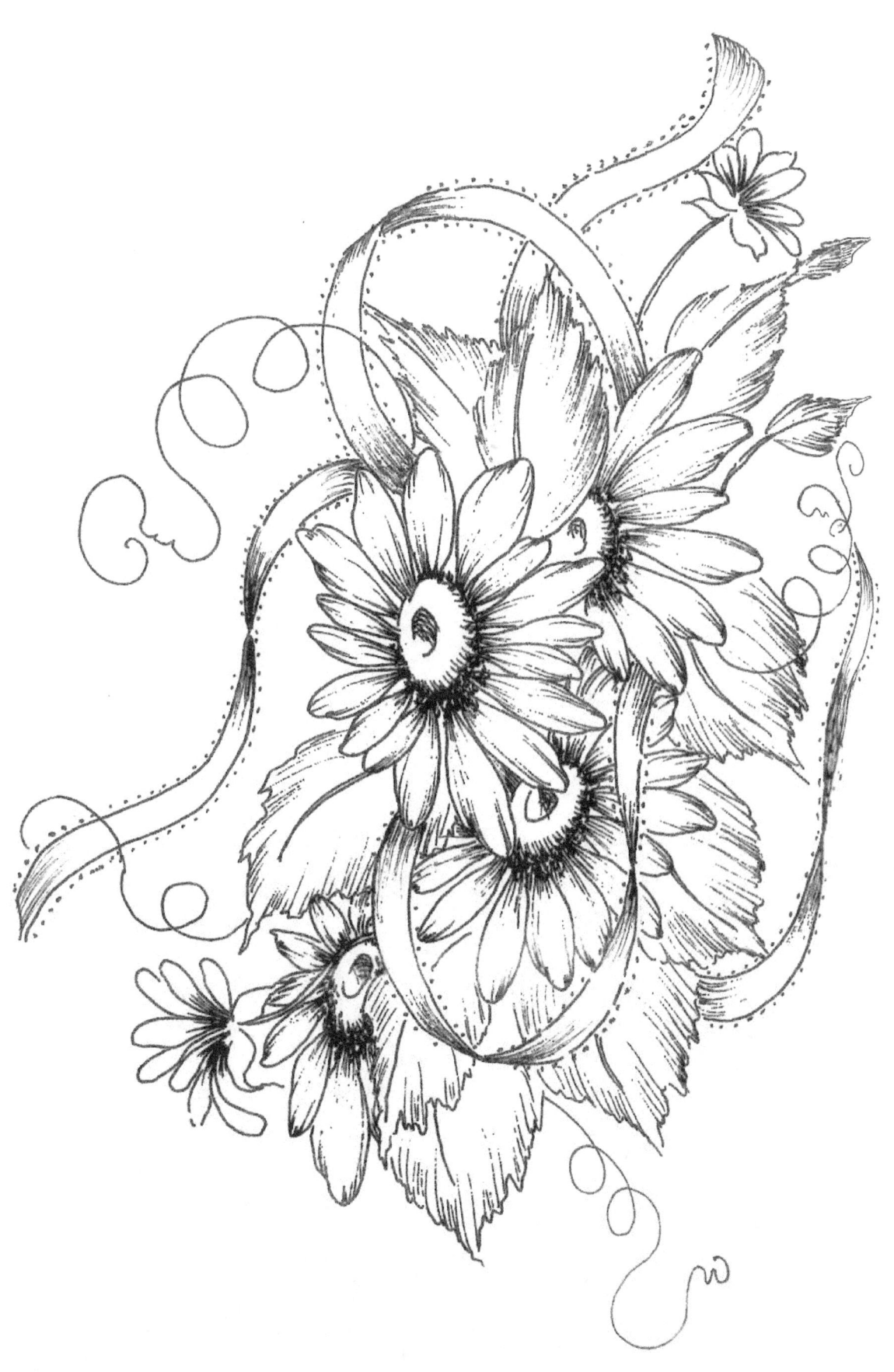

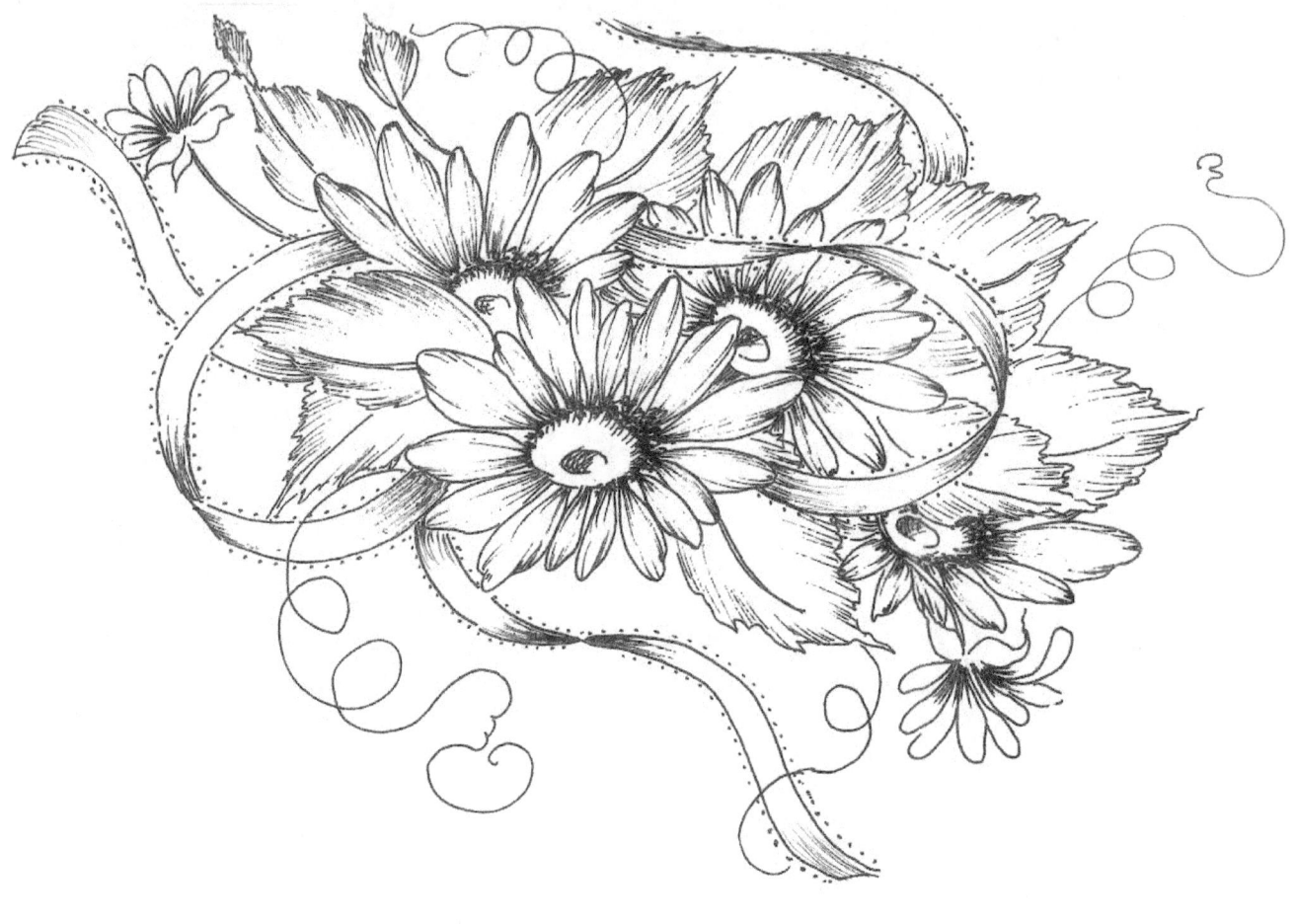

This card has been designed

with care and love especially

for you. It is suitable for framing.

Original drawing by

Louise Jackson, M.D.A.

Artistically colored by

_____

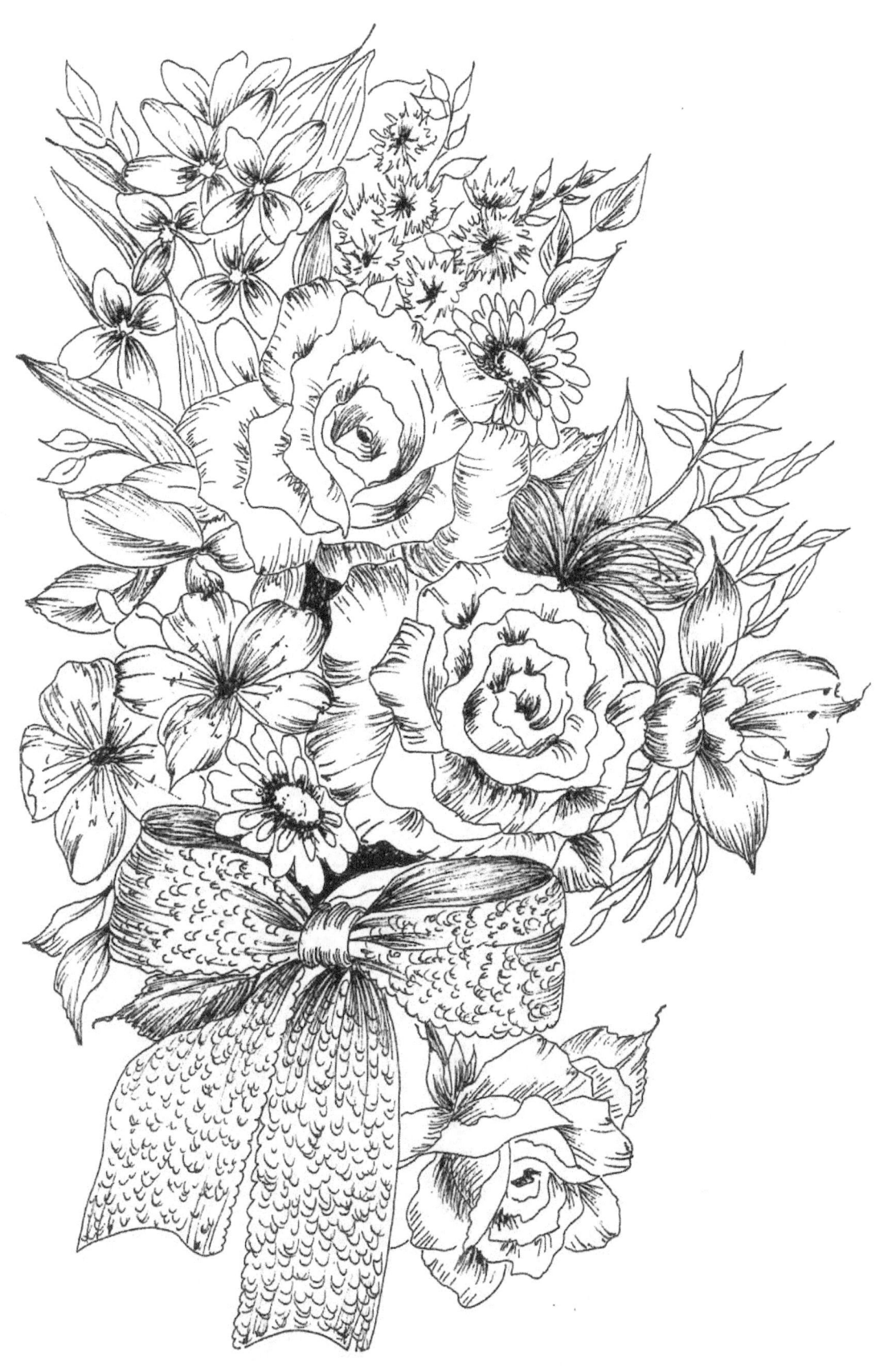

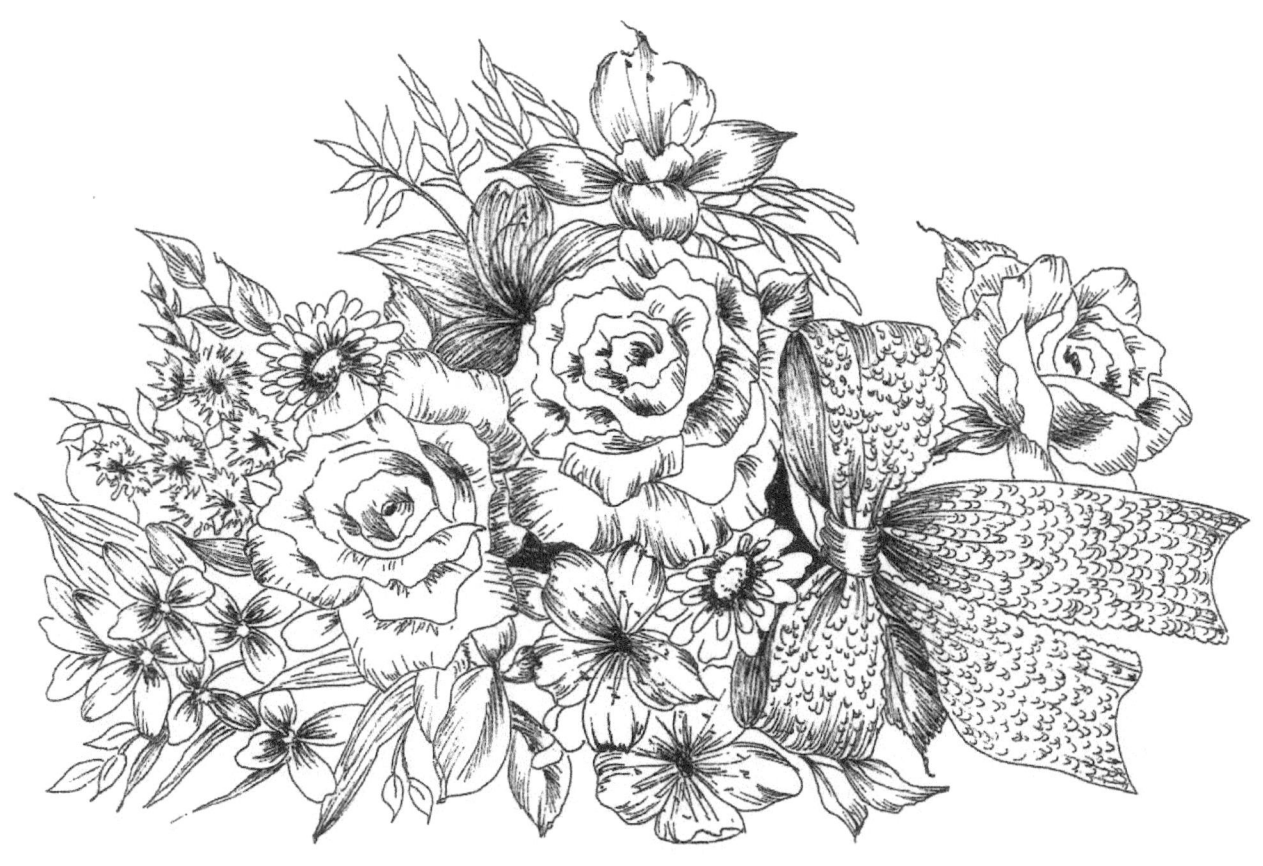

This card has been designed

with care and love especially

for you. It is suitable for framing.

Original drawing by

Louise Jackson, M.D.A.

Artistically colored by

_____

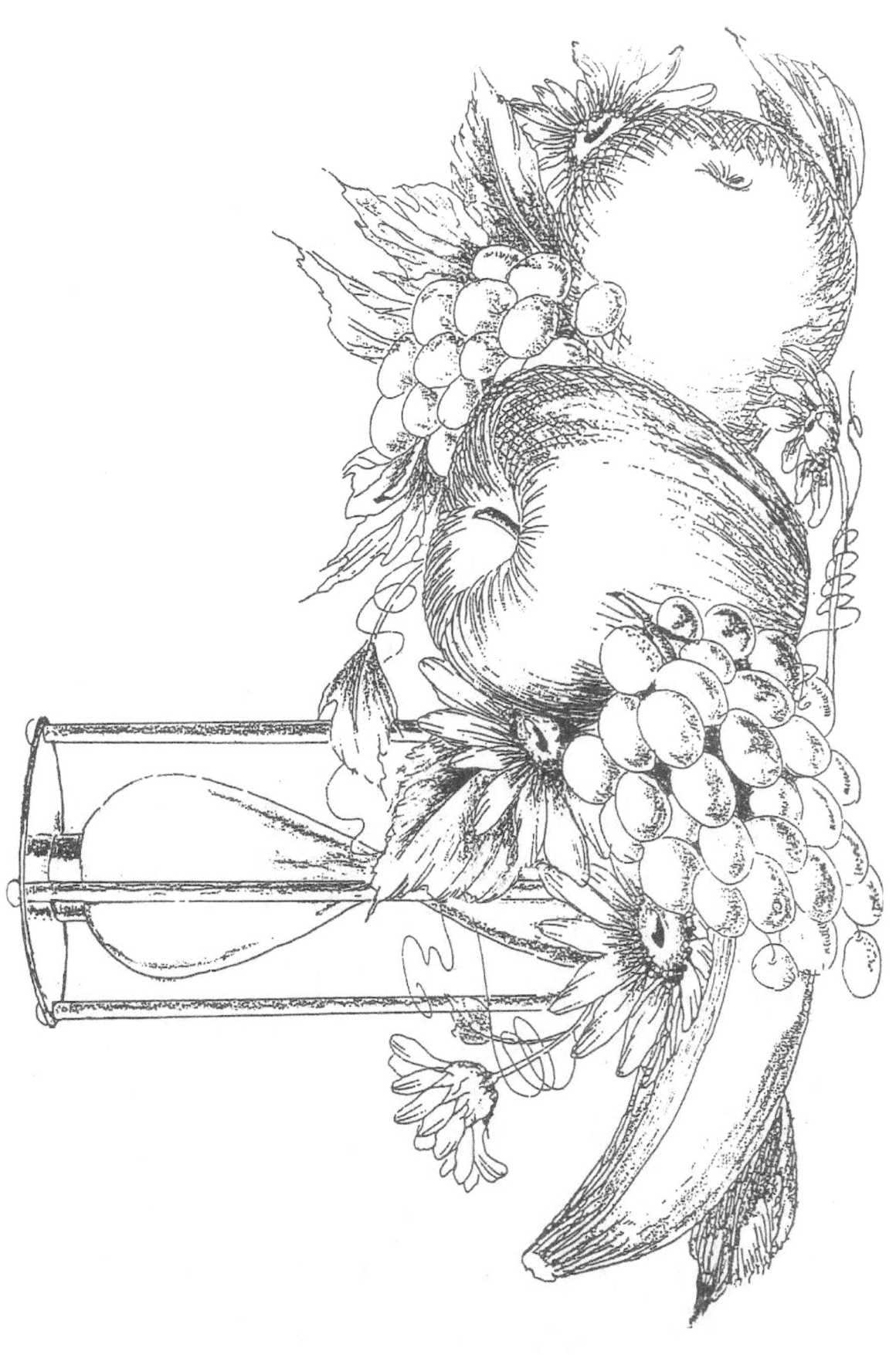

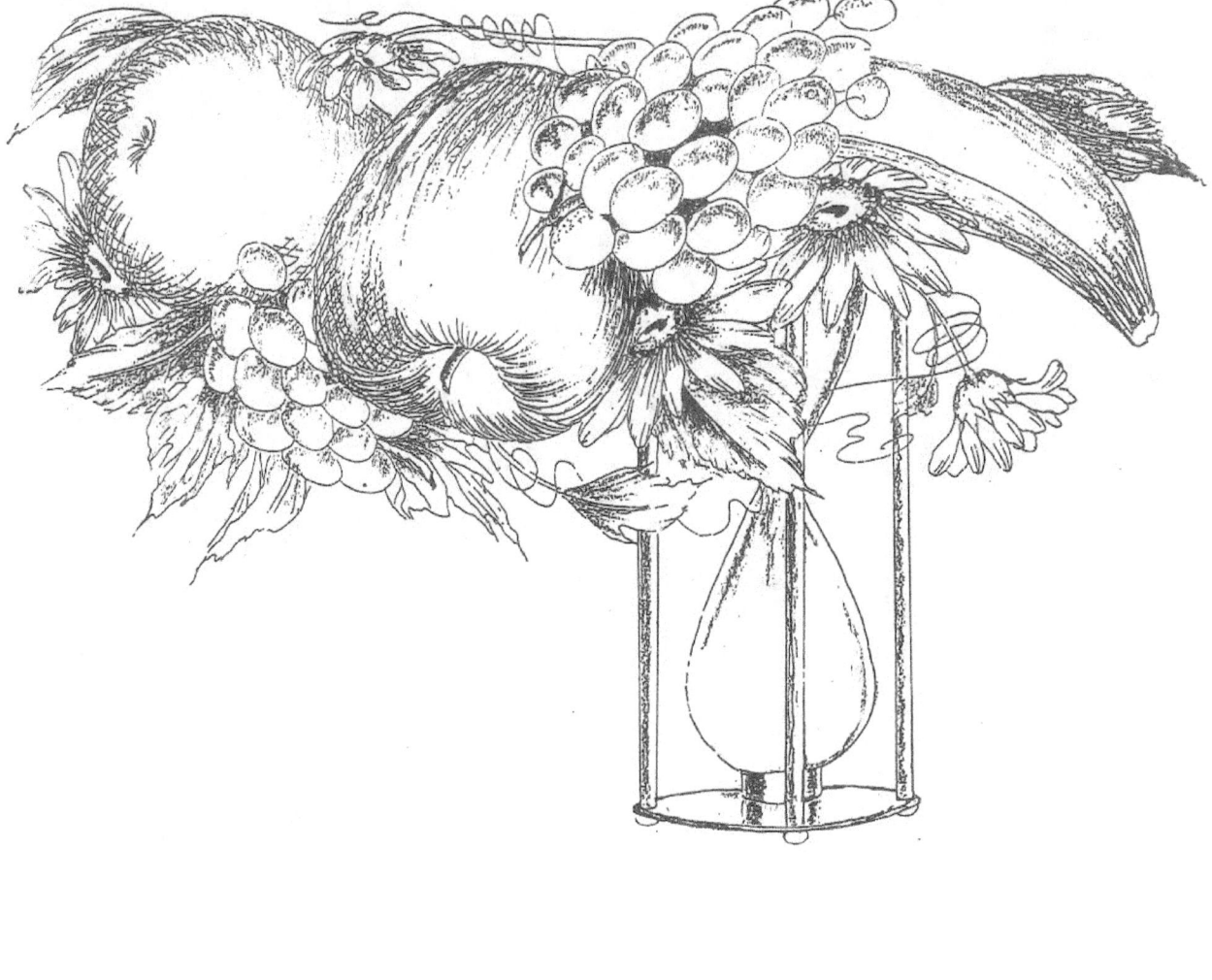

This card has been designed

with care and love especially

for you. It is suitable for framing.

Original drawing by

Louise Jackson, M.D.A.

Artistically colored by

_____

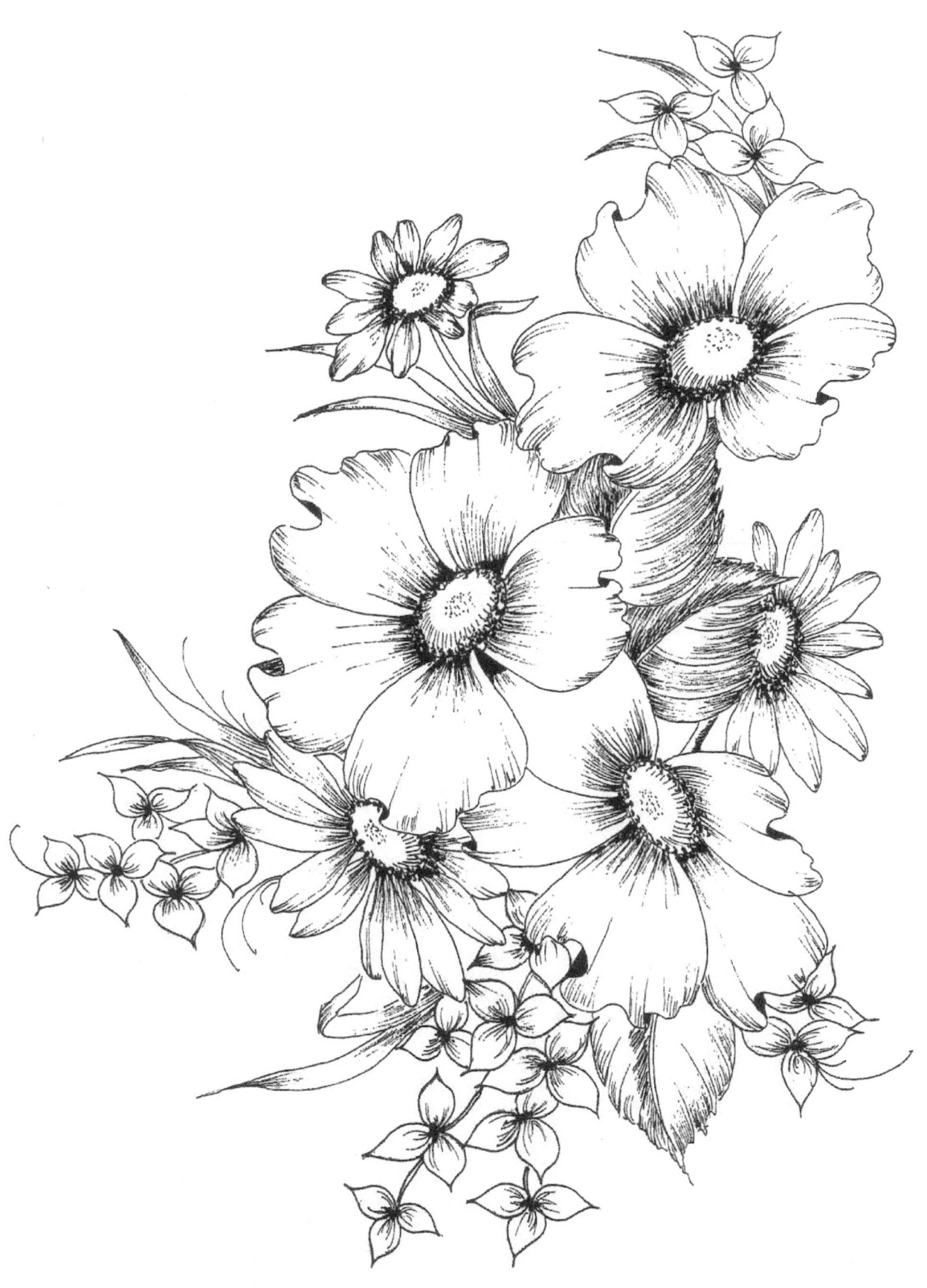

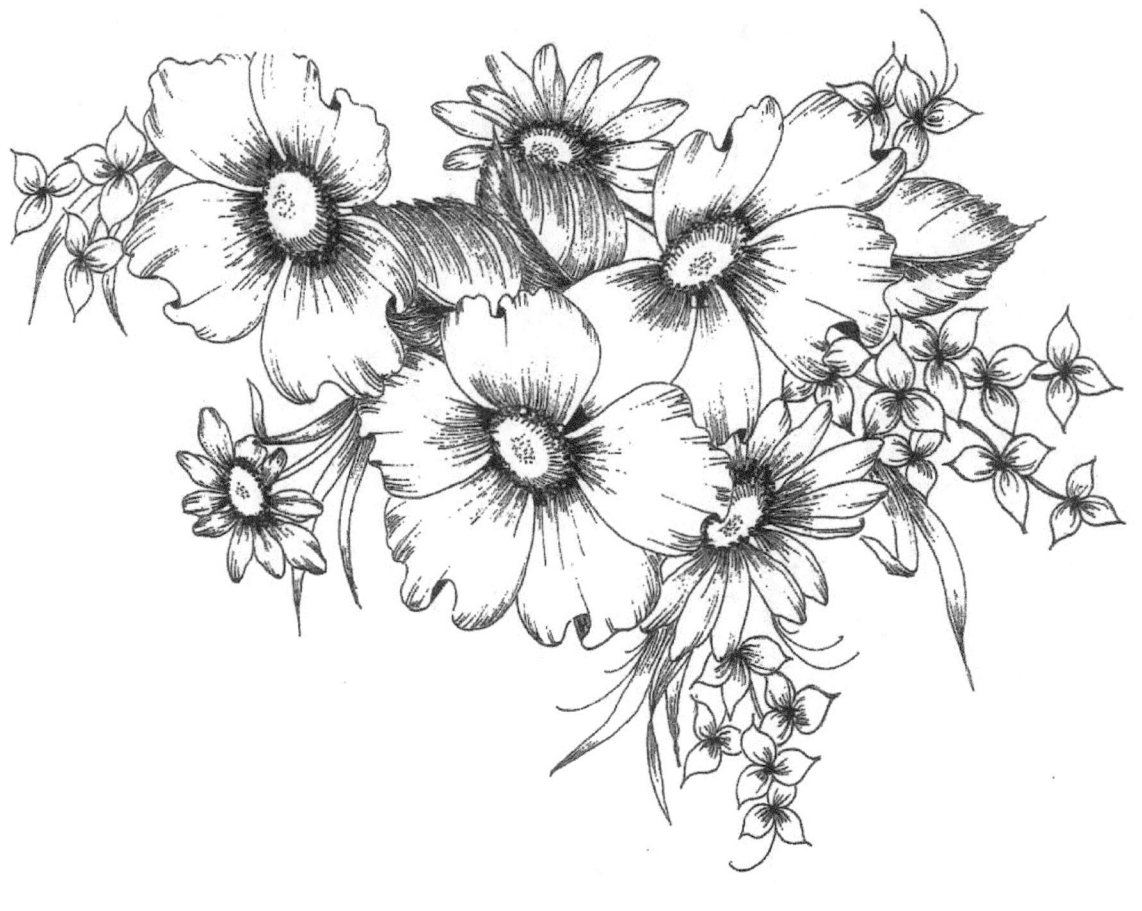

This card has been designed

with care and love.

It is especially for you and

is suitable for framing.

Original drawing by

Louise Jackson M.D.A.

Artistically colored by

_____

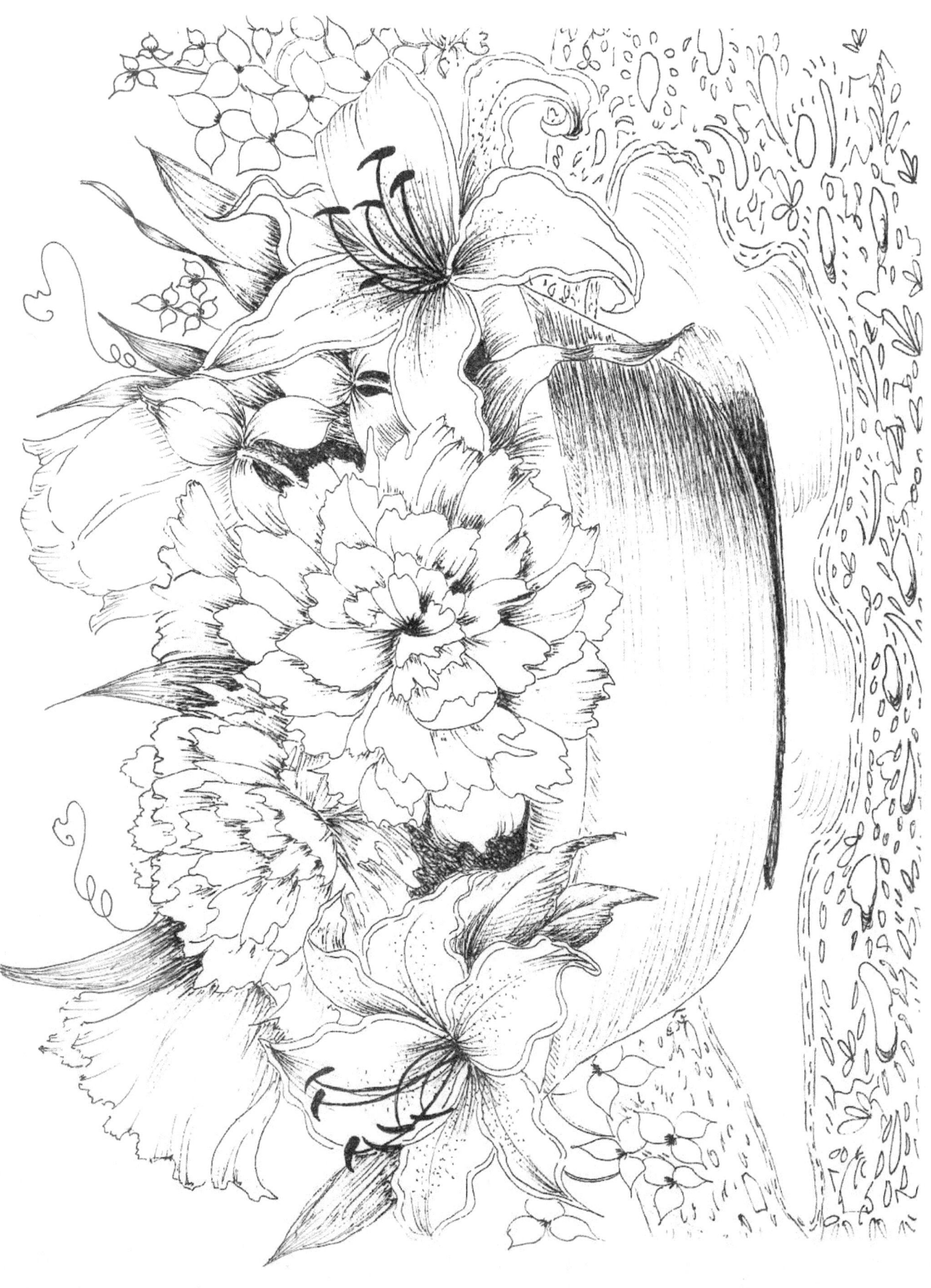

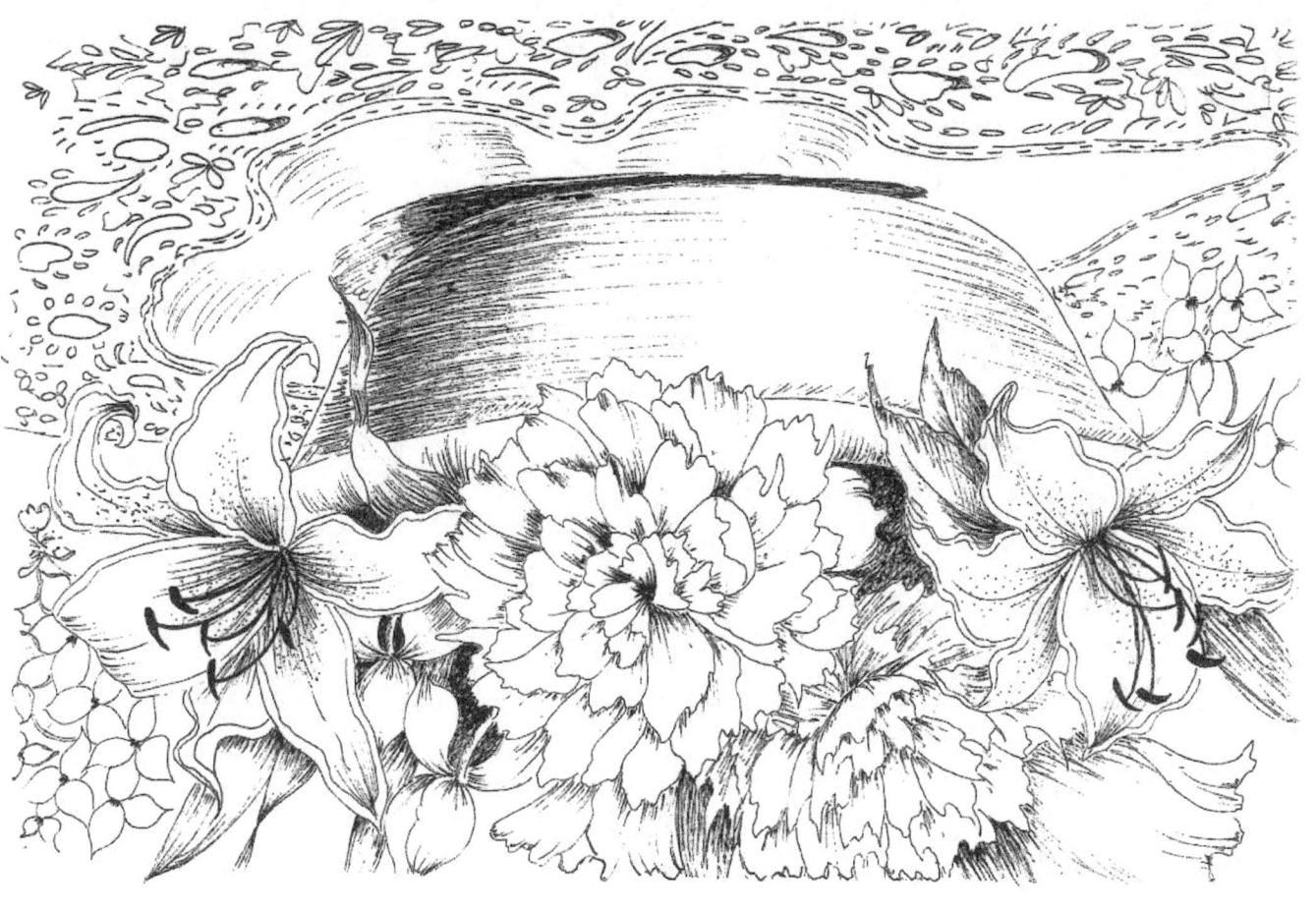

This card has been designed

with care and love especially

for you. It is suitable for framing.

Original drawing by

Louise Jackson, M.D.A.

Artistically colored by

_____

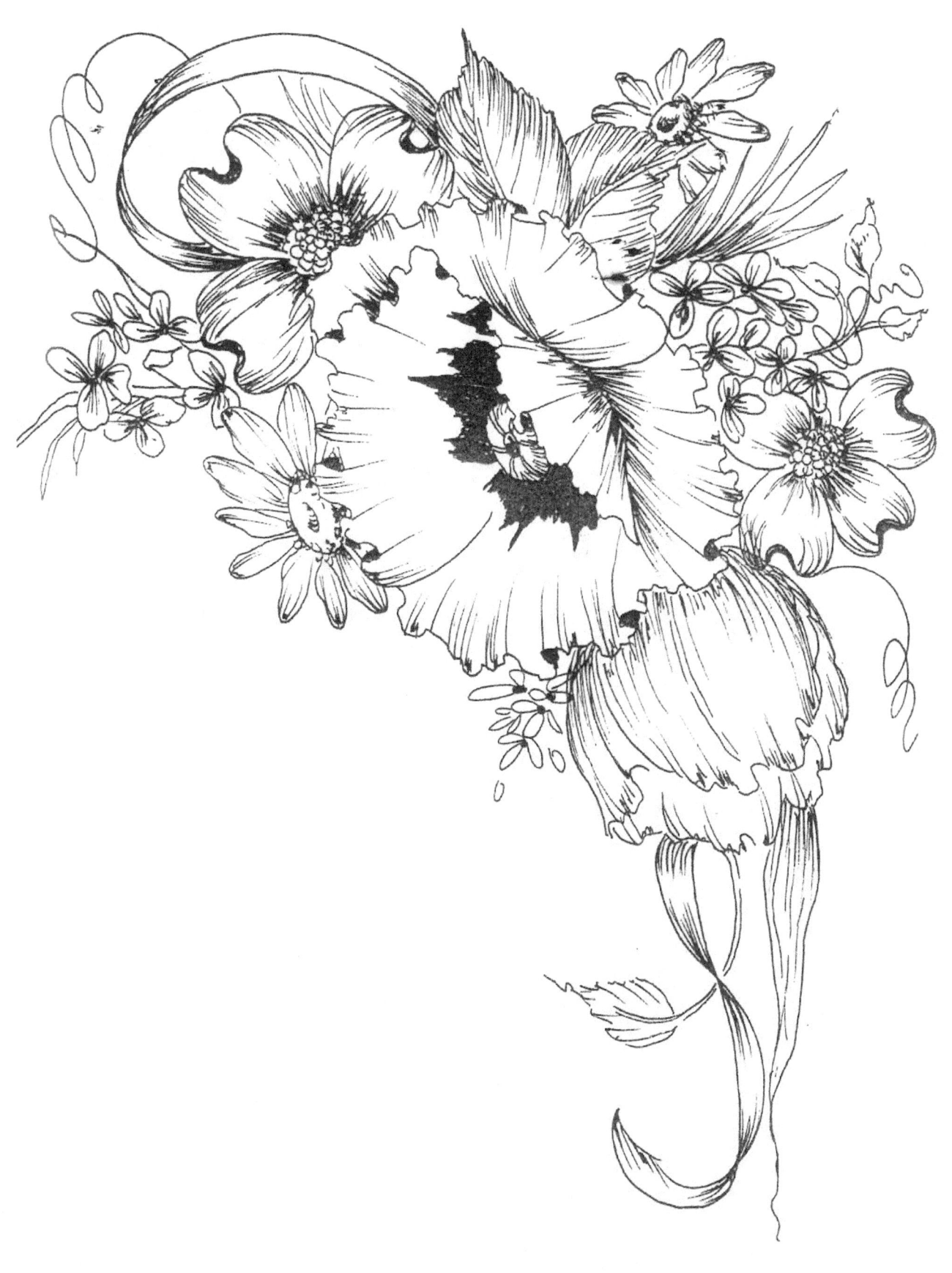

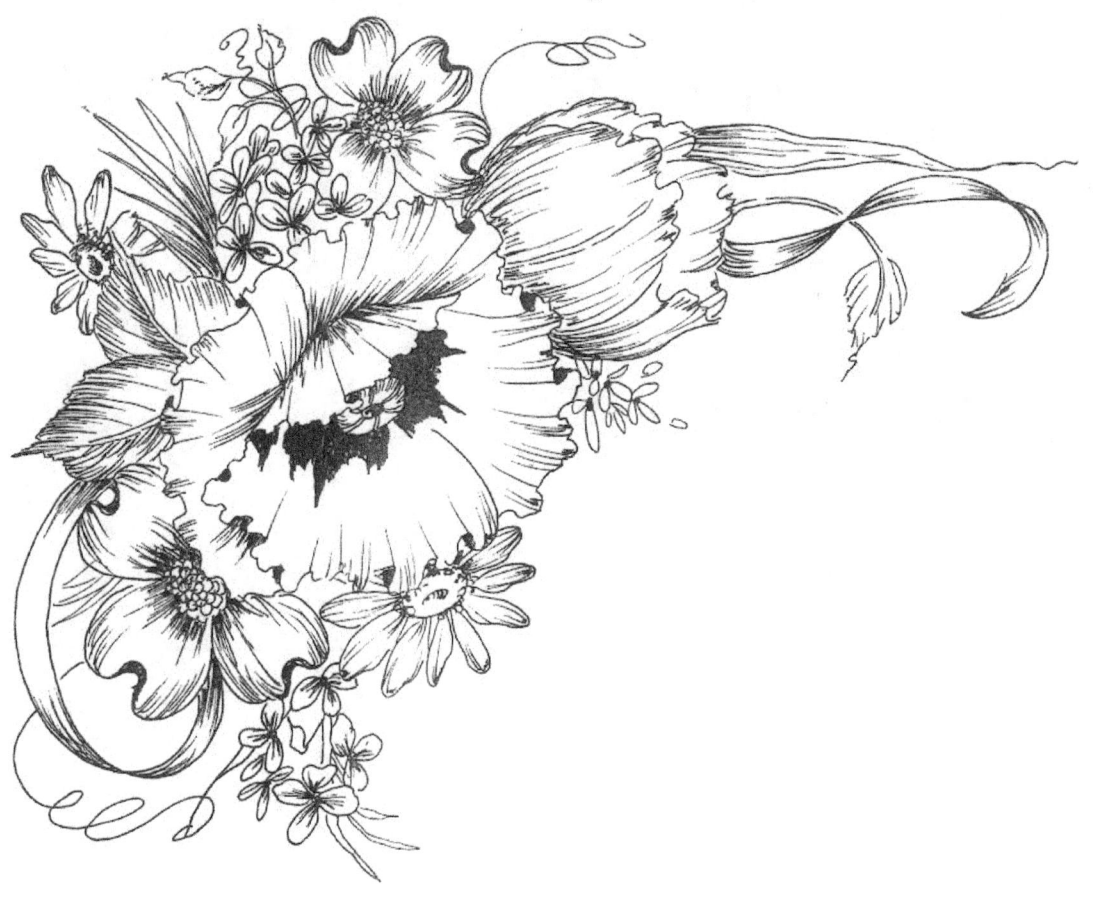

This card has been designed

with care and love especially

for you. It is suitable for framing.

Original drawing by

Louise Jackson, M.D.A.

Artistically colored by

_____

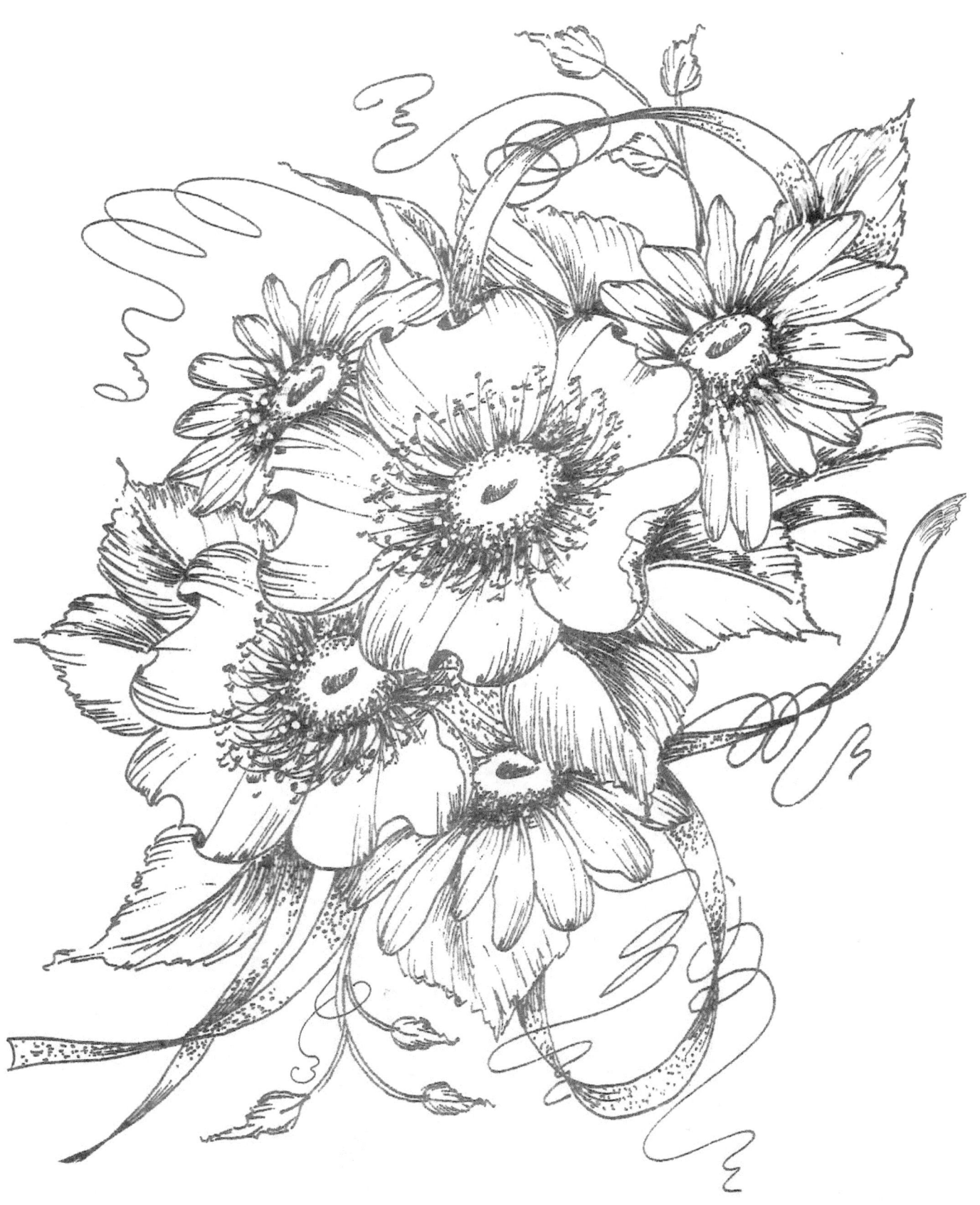

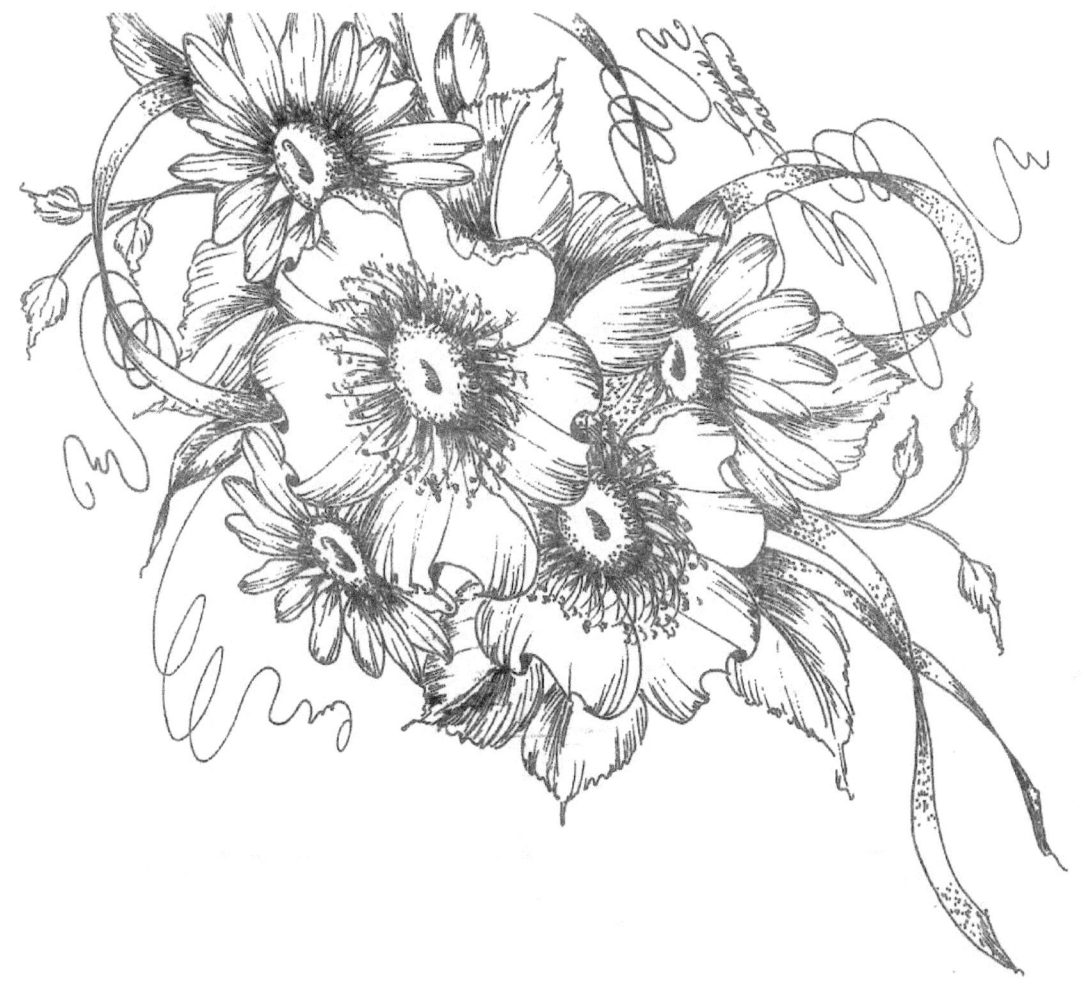

This card has been designed

with care and love especially

for you. It is suitable for framing.

Original drawing by

Louise Jackson, M.D.A.

Artistically colored by

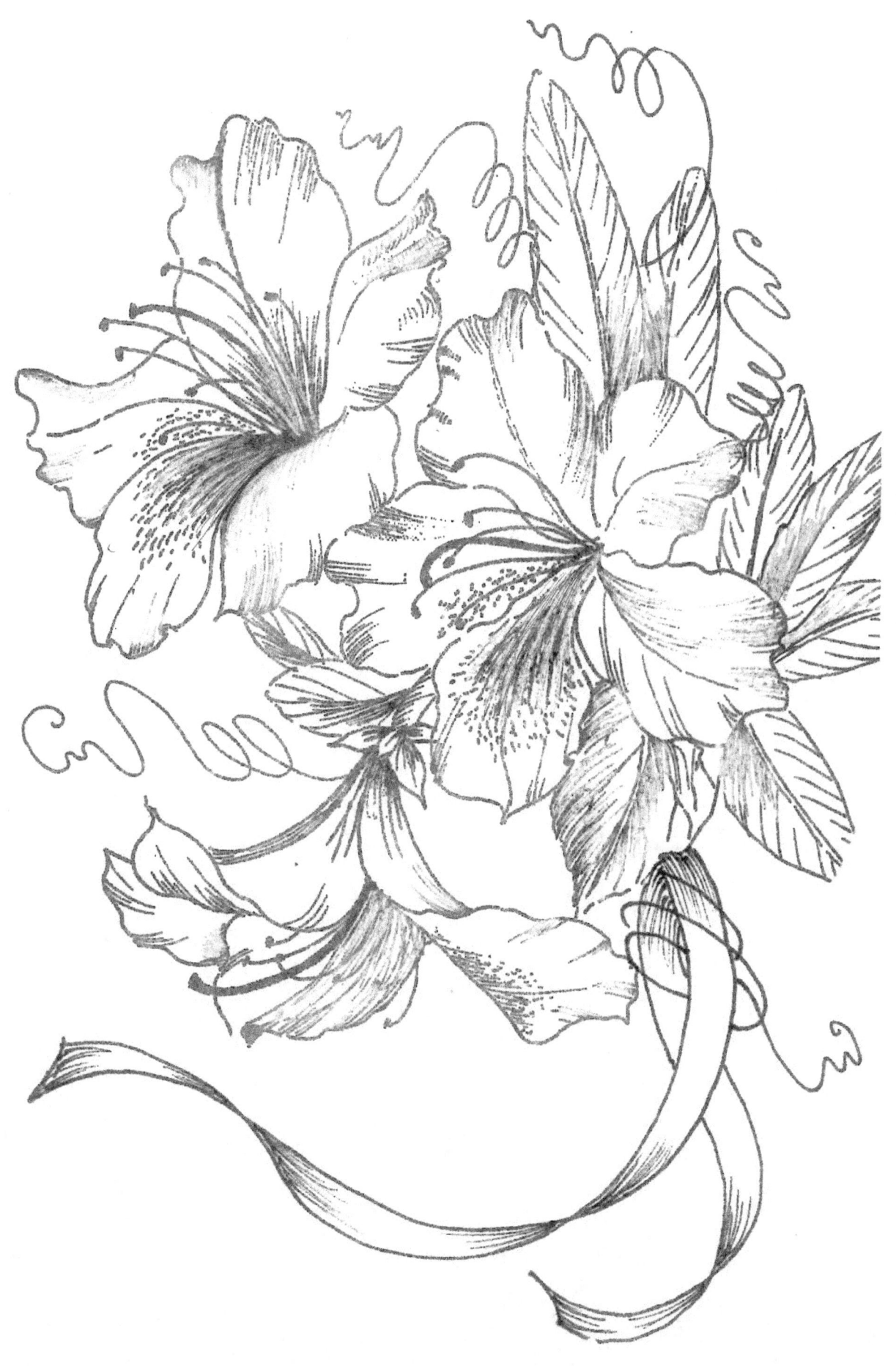

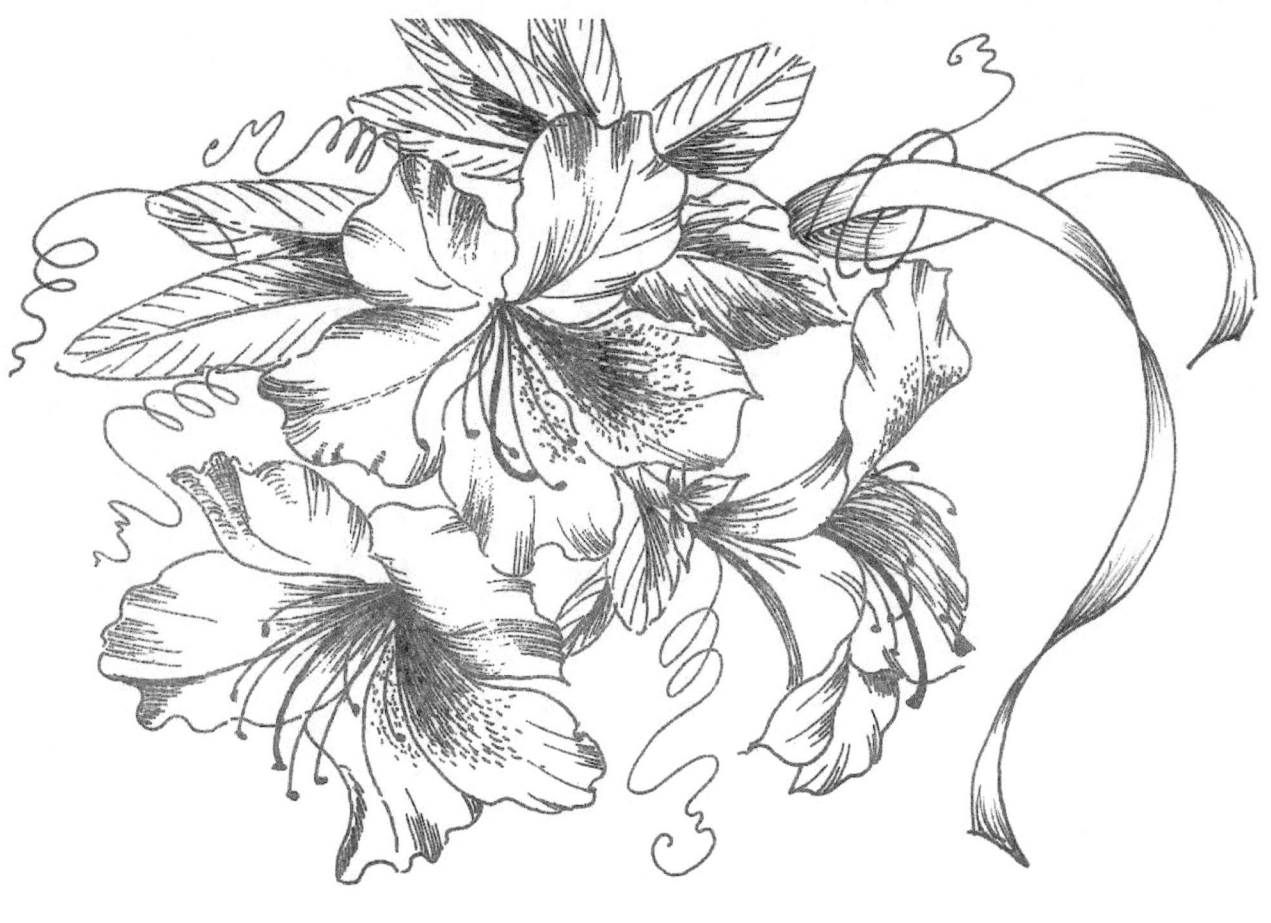

This card has been designed

with care and love especially

for you. It is suitable for framing.

Original drawing by

Louise Jackson, M.D.A.

Artistically colored by

_____

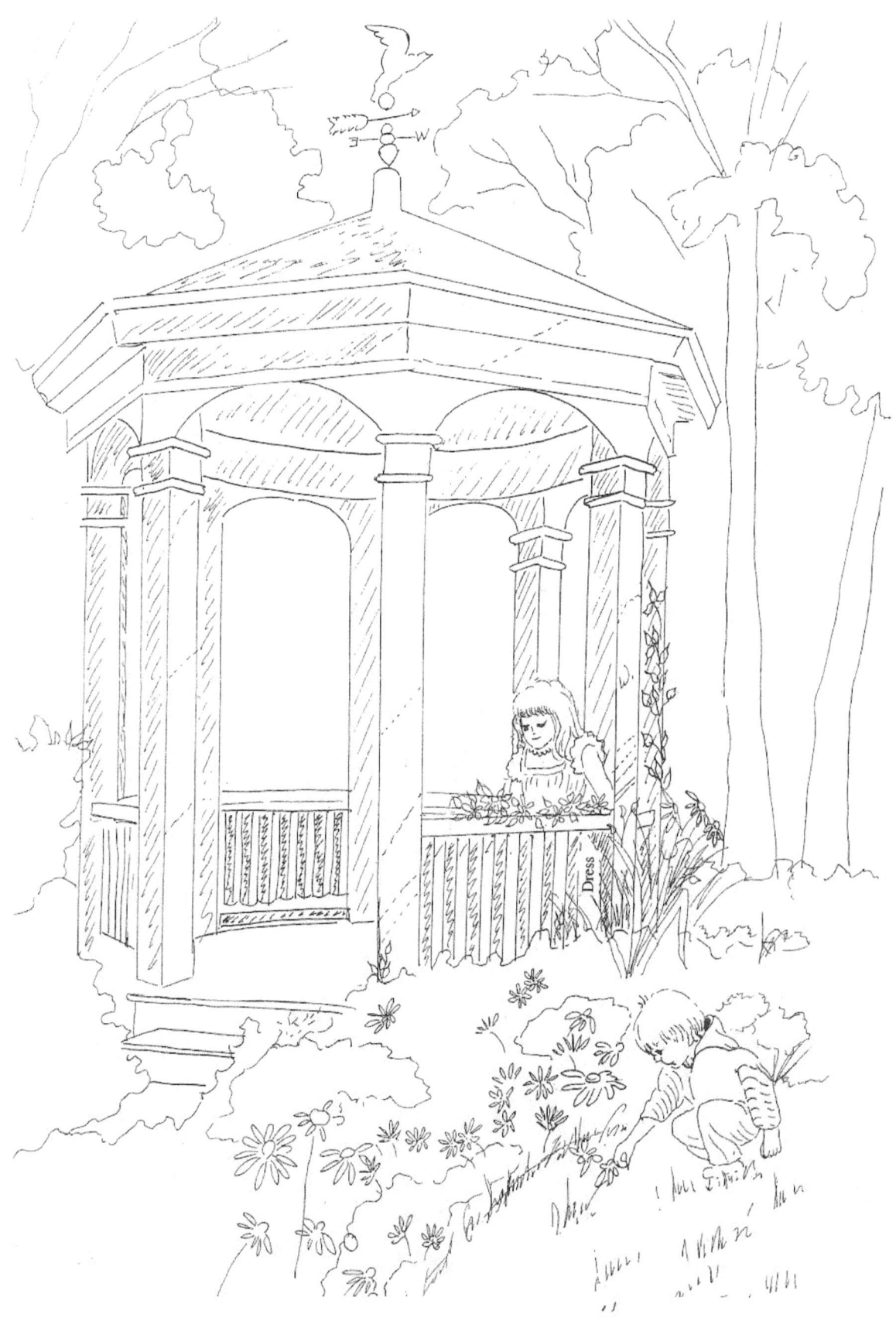

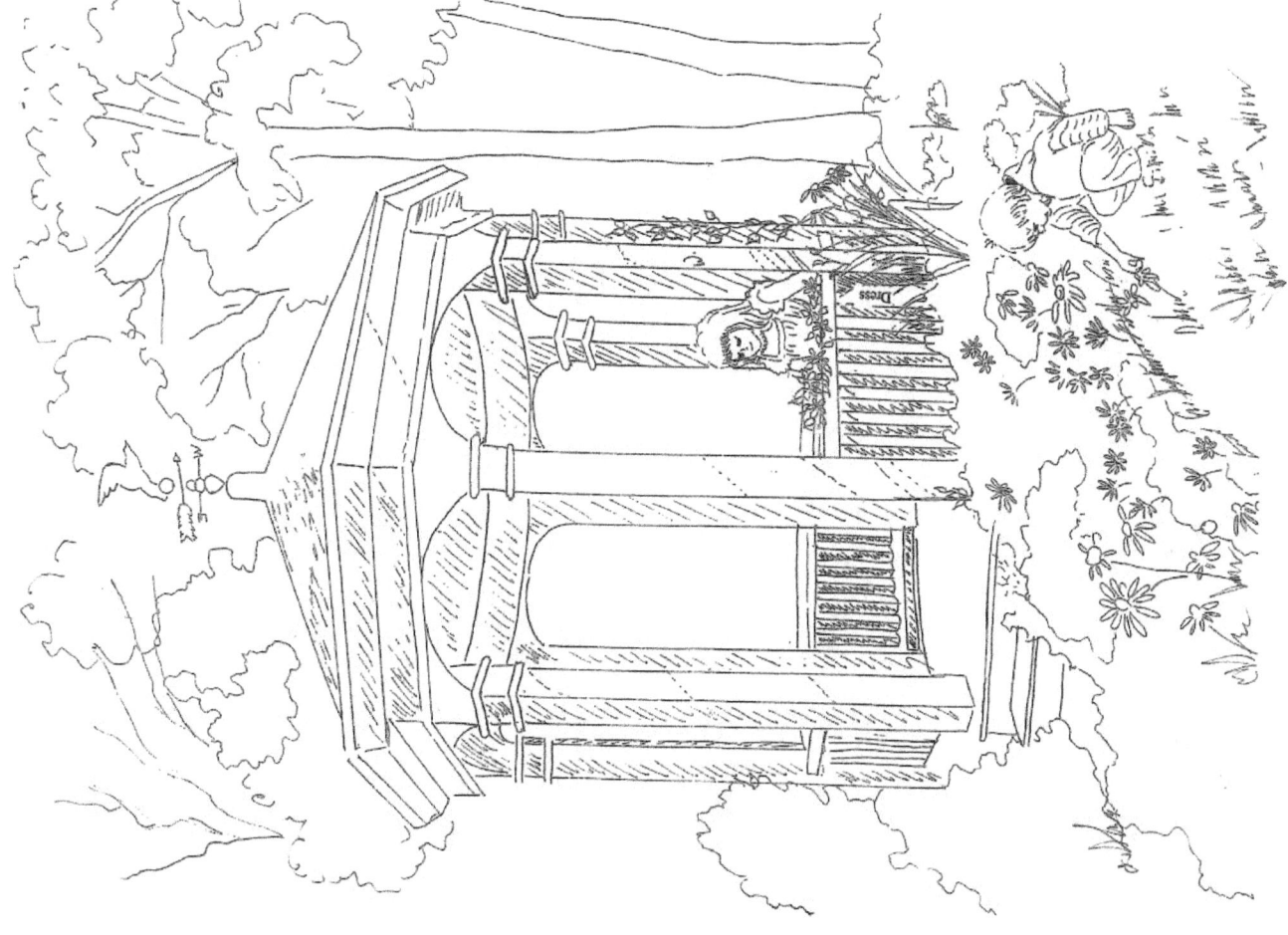

This card has been designed

with care and love especially

for you. It is suitable for framing.

Original drawing by

Louise Jackson, M.D.A.

Artistically colored by

_____

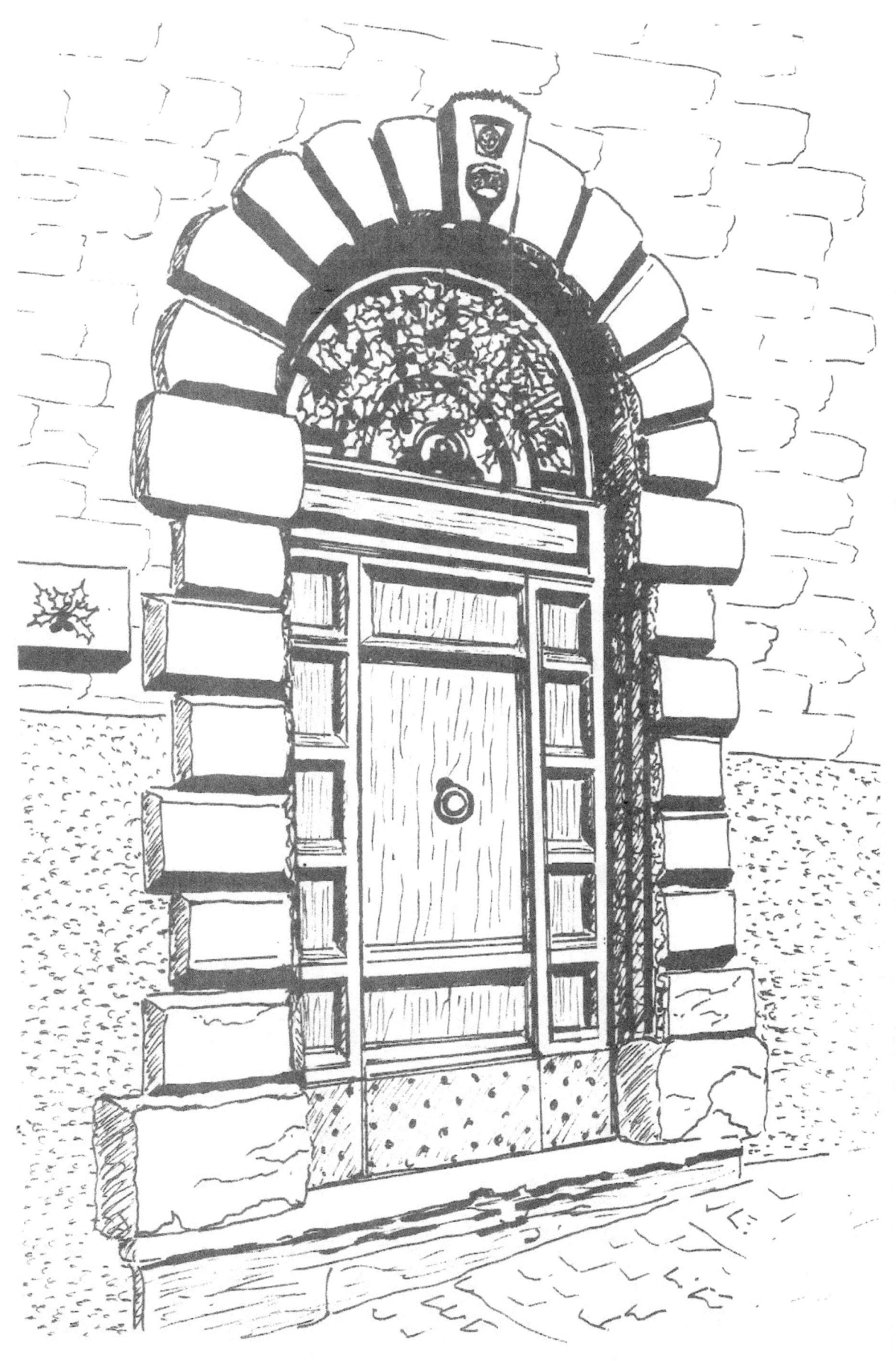

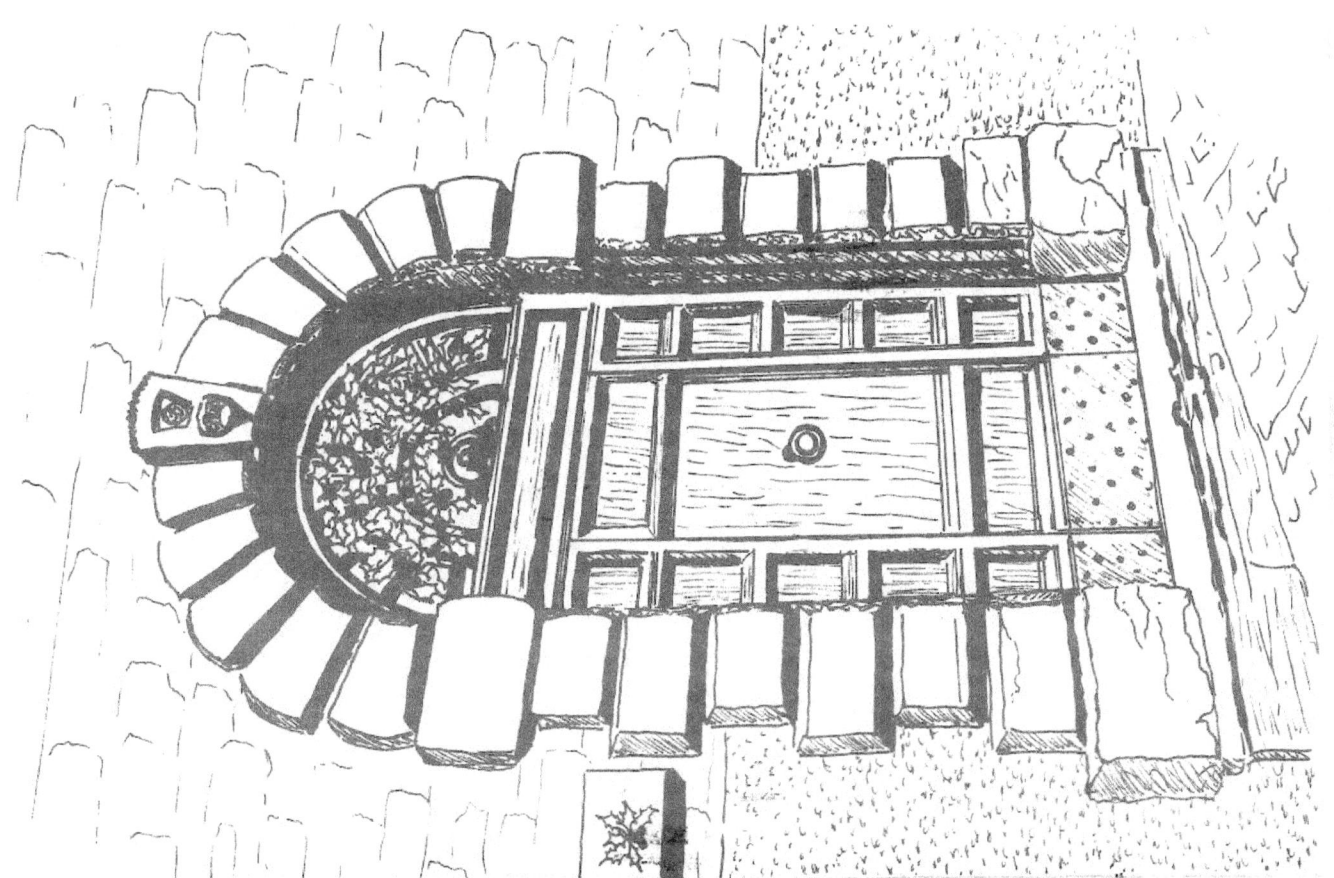

This card has been designed
with care and love especially
for you. It is suitable for framing.

Original drawing by

Louise Jackson, M.D.A.

Artistically colored by

_____

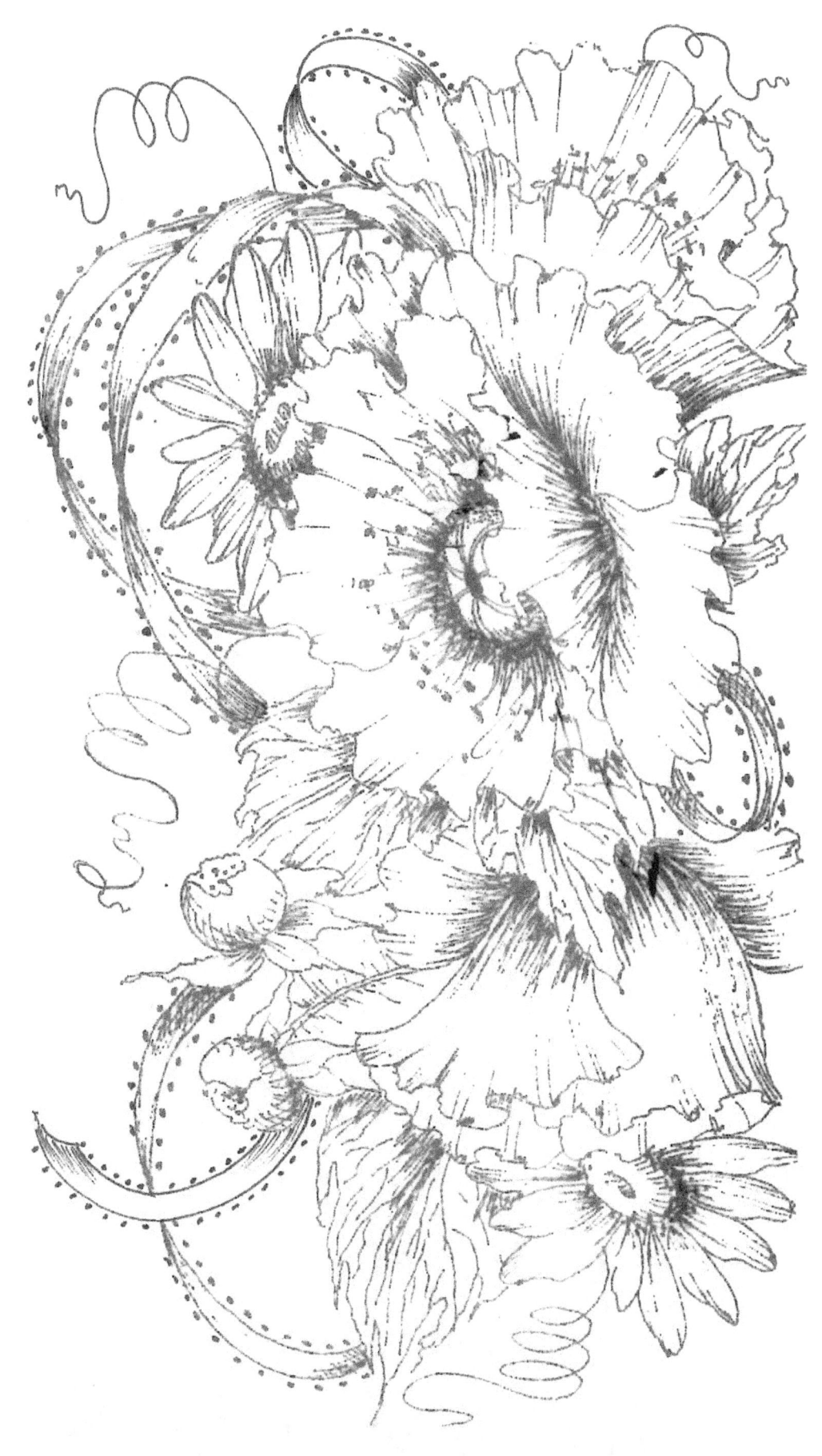

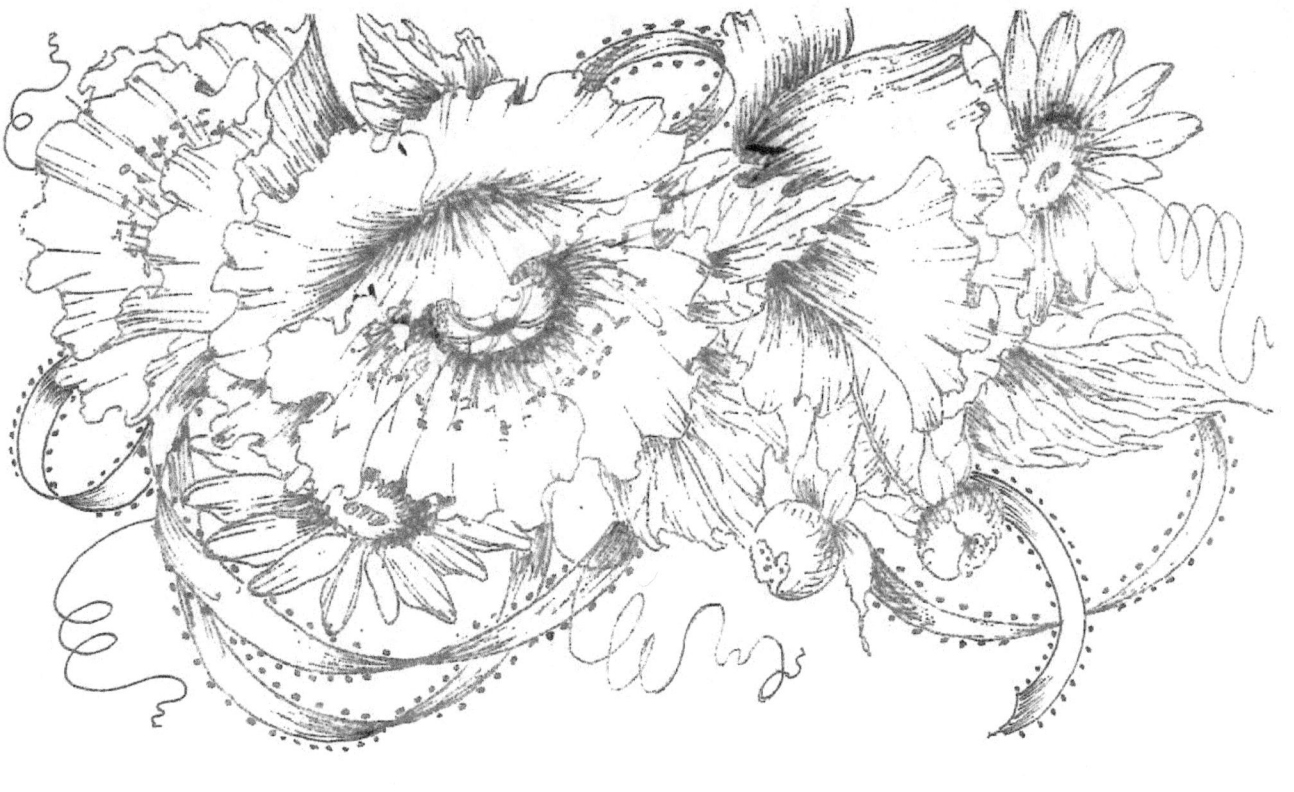

This card has been designed

with care and love especially

for you. It is suitable for framing.

Original drawing by

Louise Jackson, M.D.A.

Artistically colored by

_____

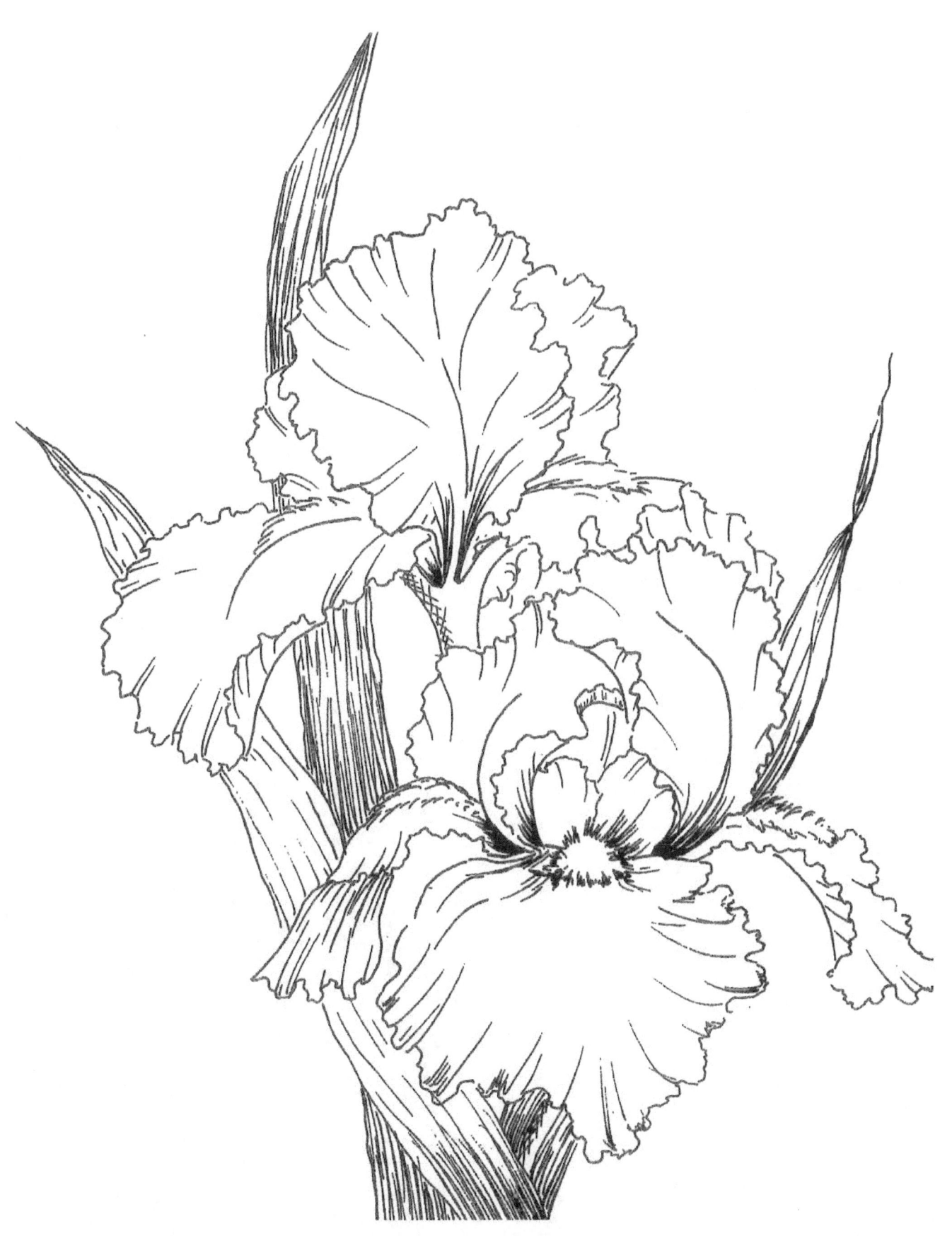

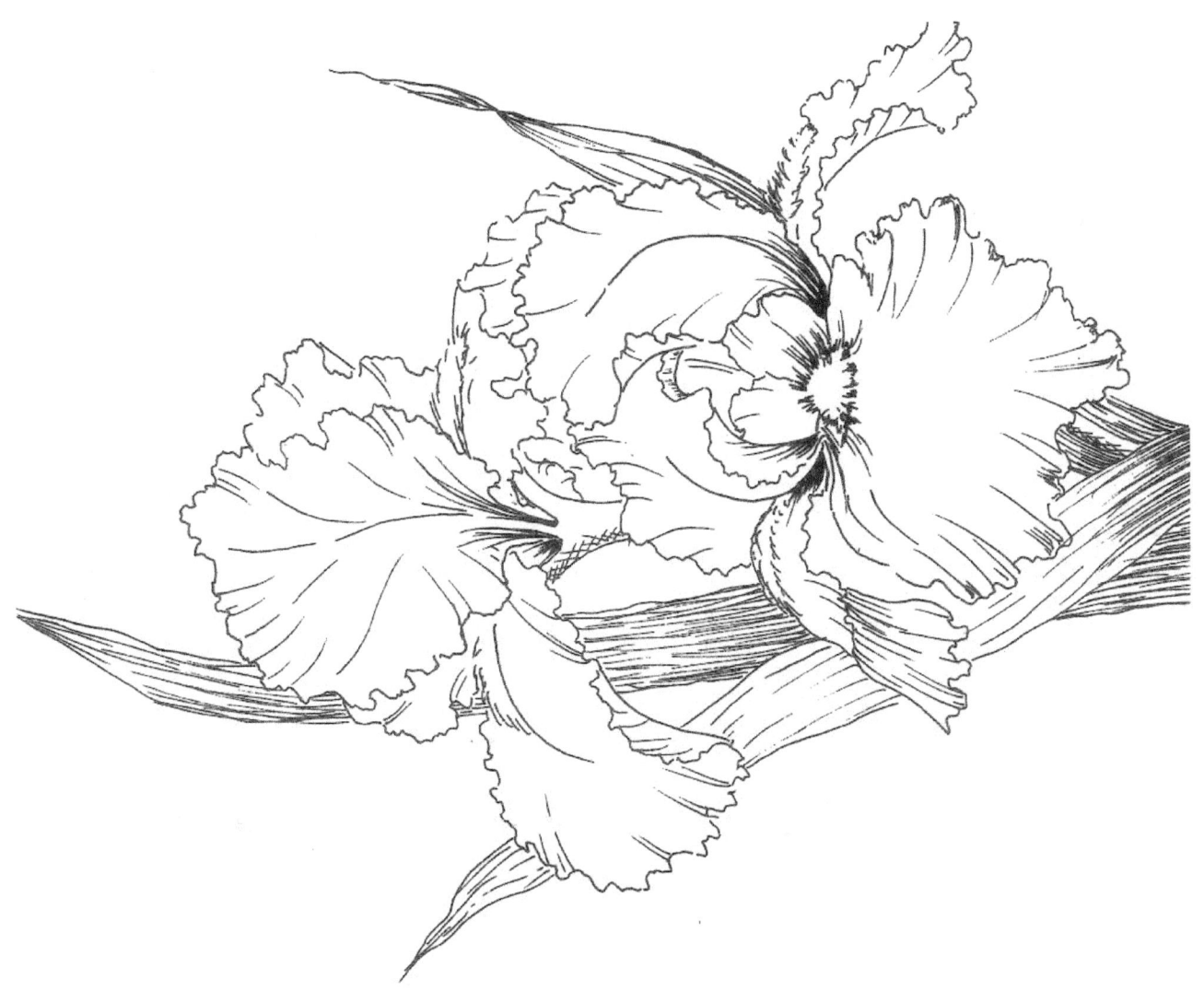

This card has been designed

with care and love especially

for you. It is suitable for framing.

Original drawing by

Louise Jackson, M.D.A.

Artistically colored by

_____

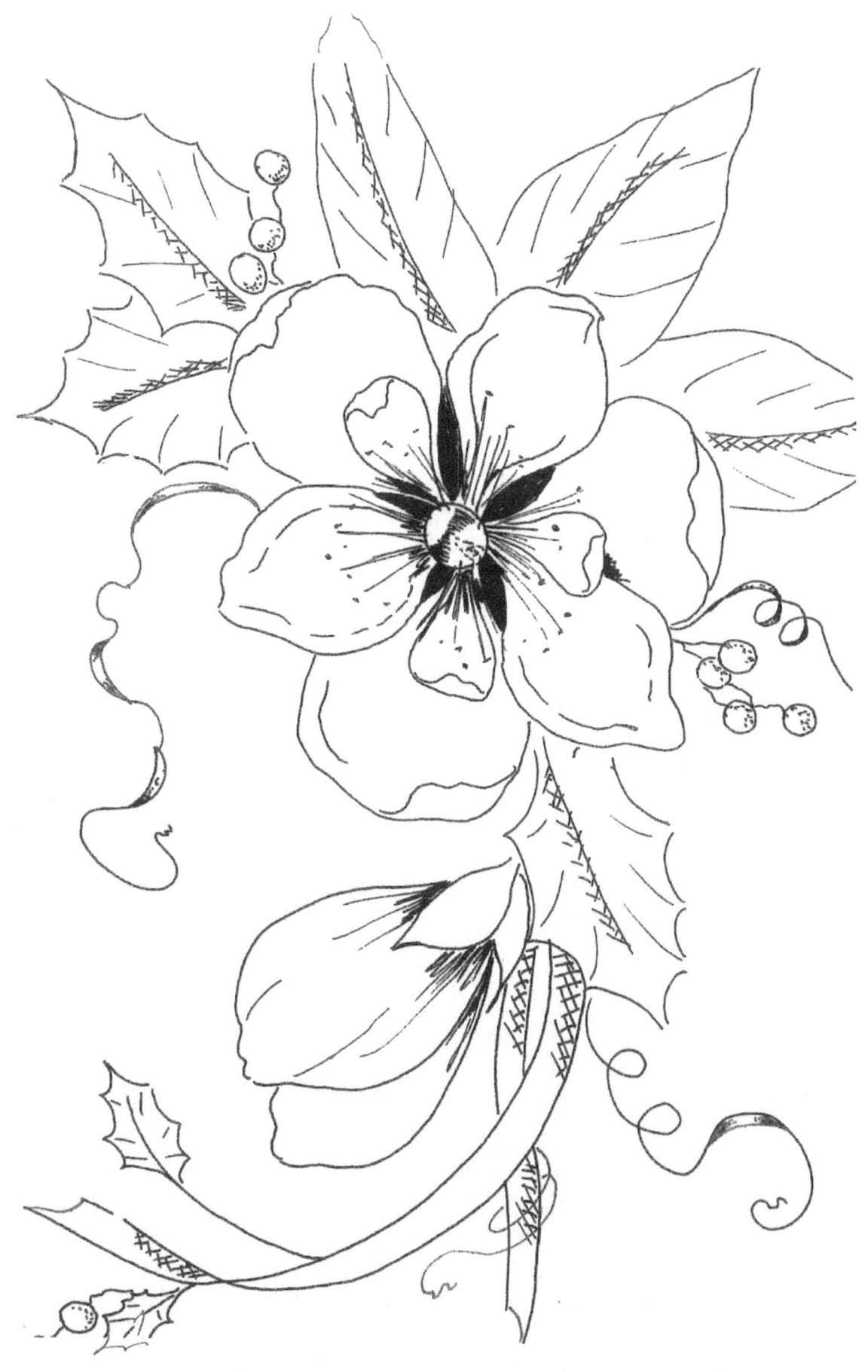

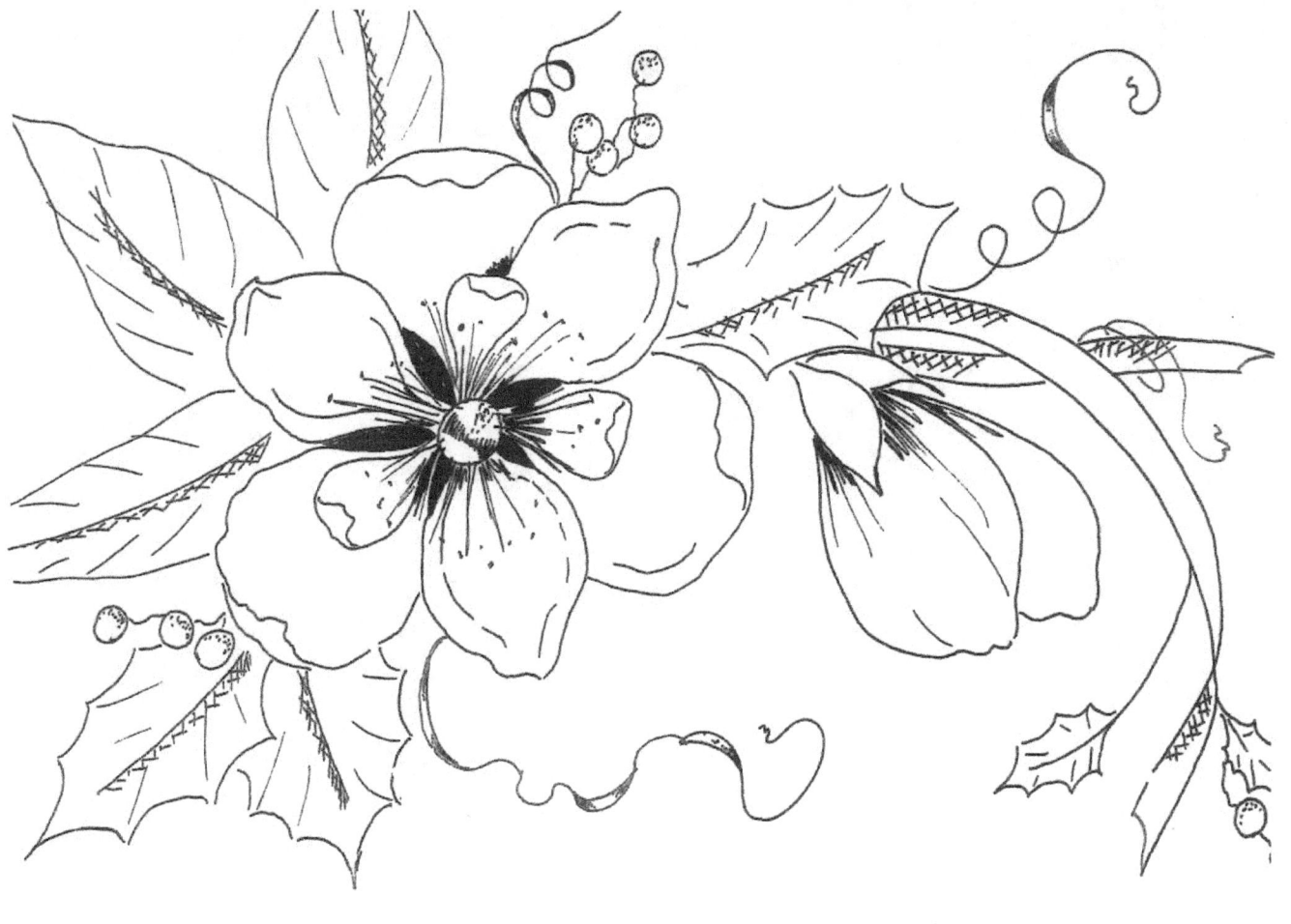

This card has been designed

with care and love especially

for you. It is suitable for framing.

Original drawing by

Louise Jackson, M.D.A.

Artistically colored by

_____

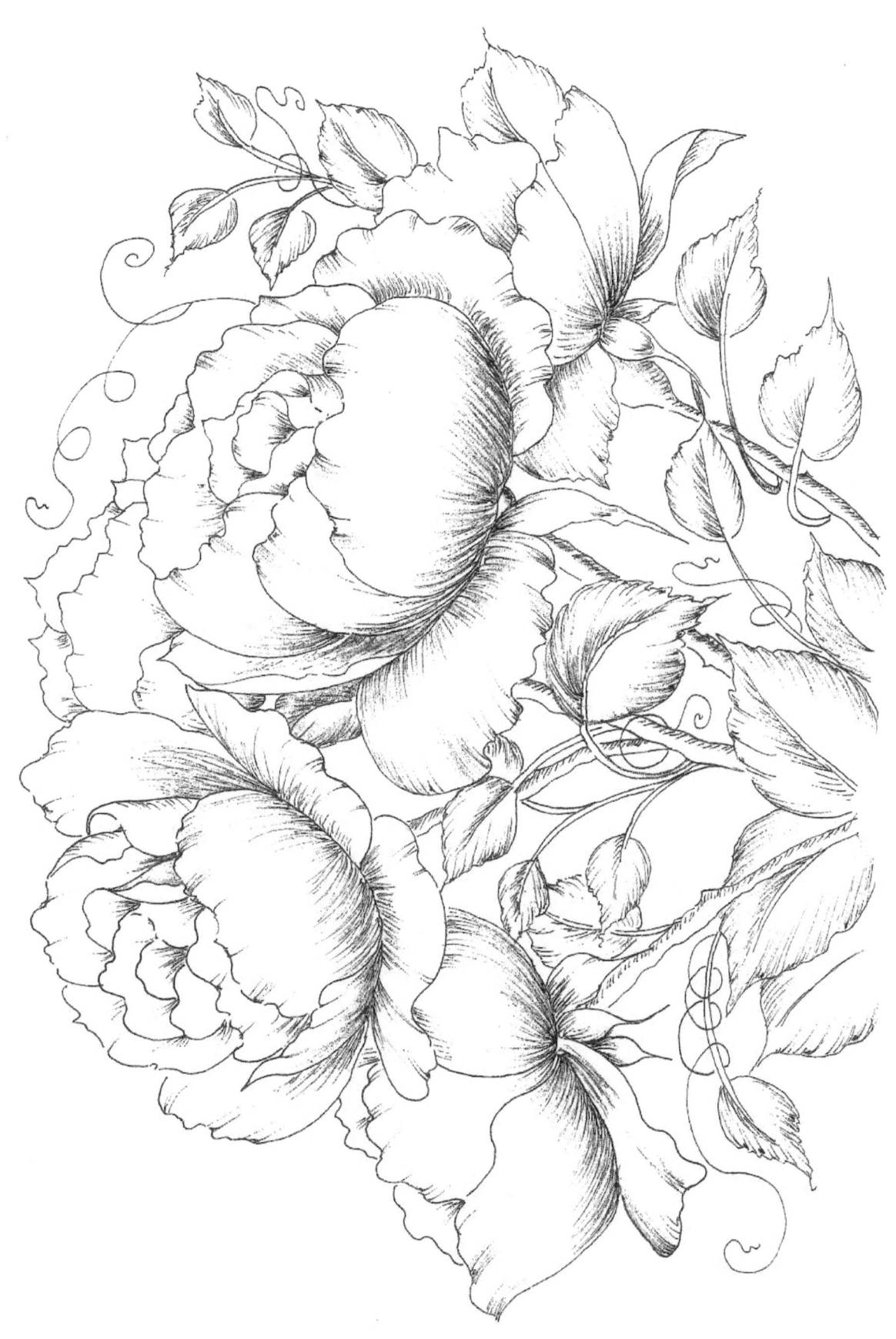

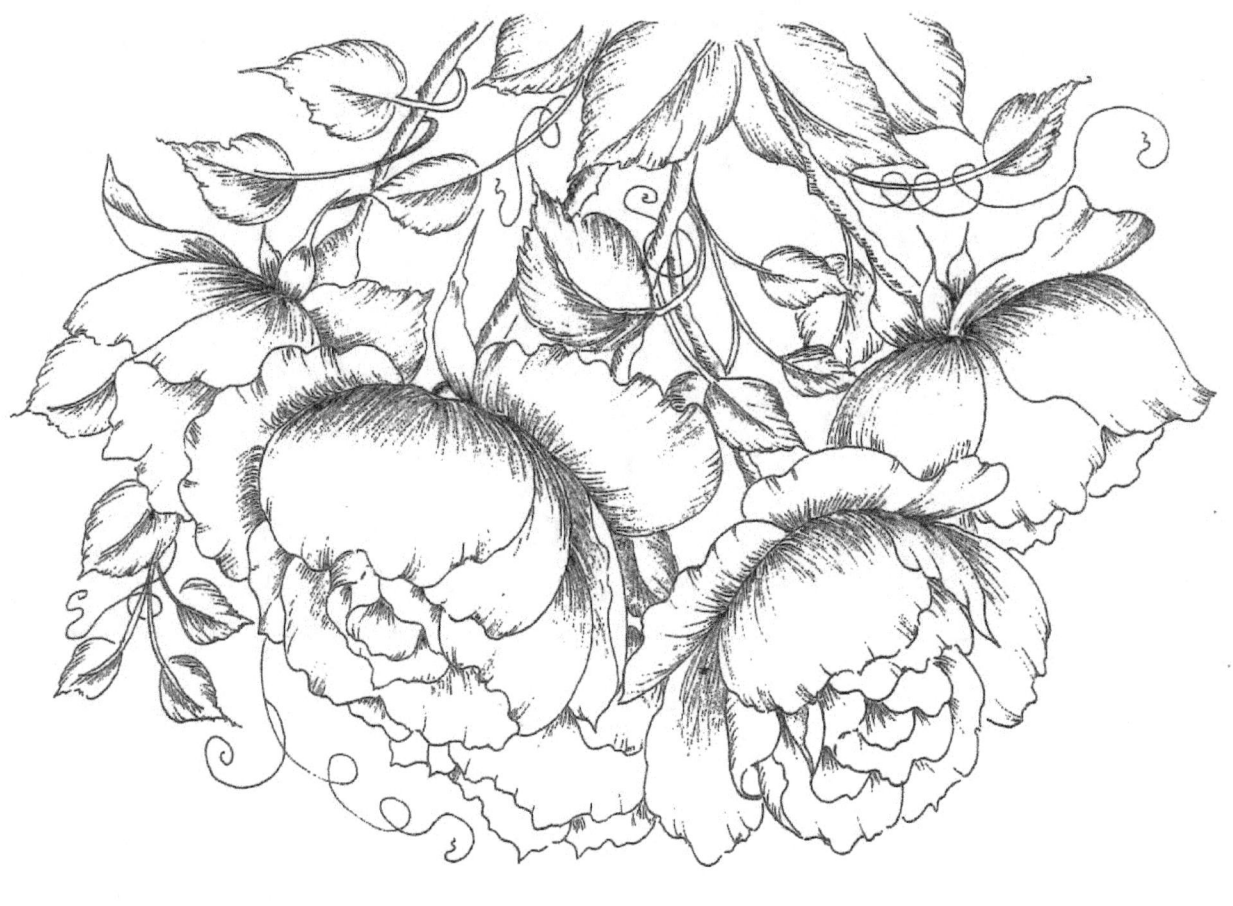

This card has been designed

with care and love especially

for you. It is suitable for framing.

Original drawing by

Louise Jackson, M.D.A.

Artistically colored by

_____

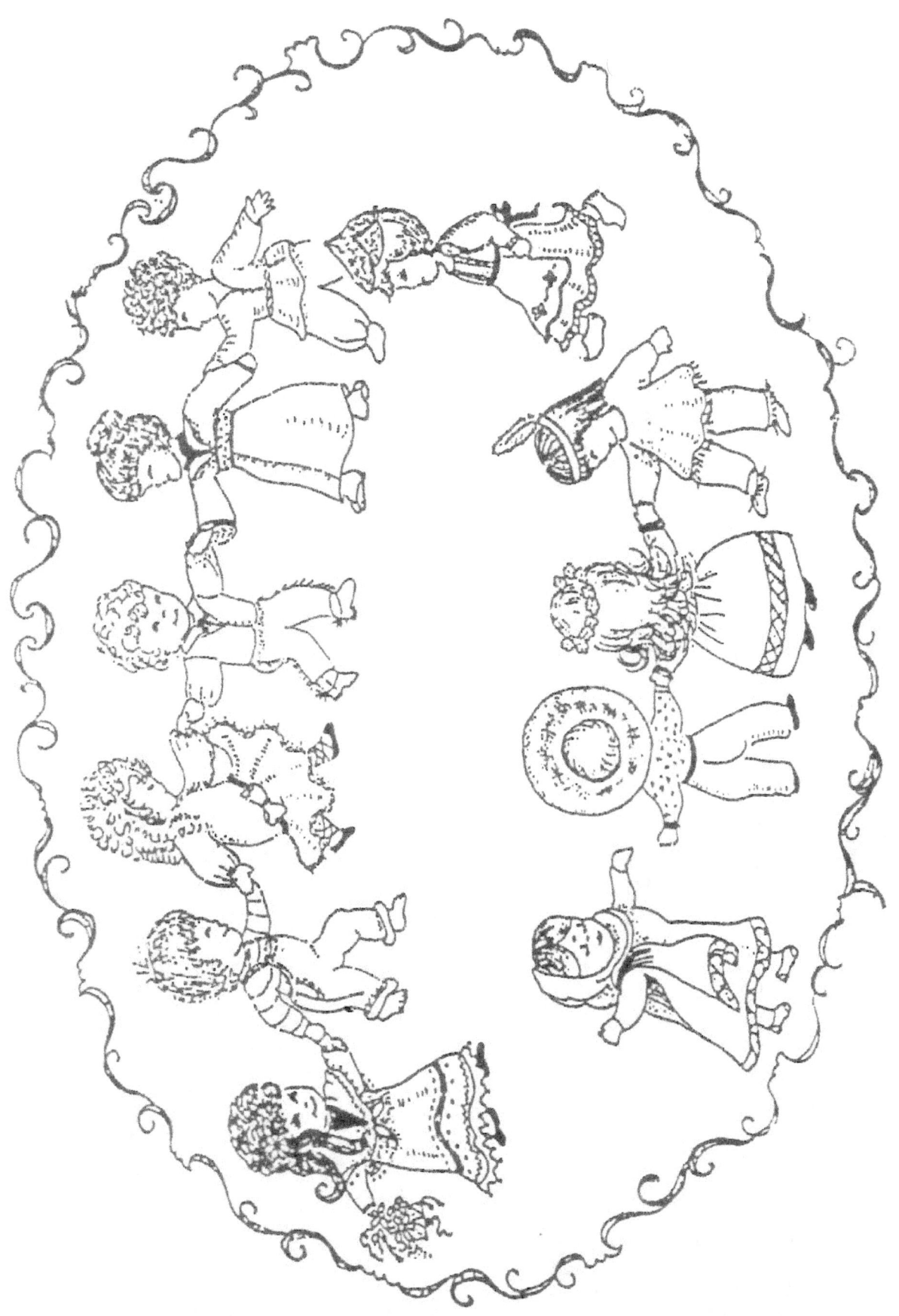

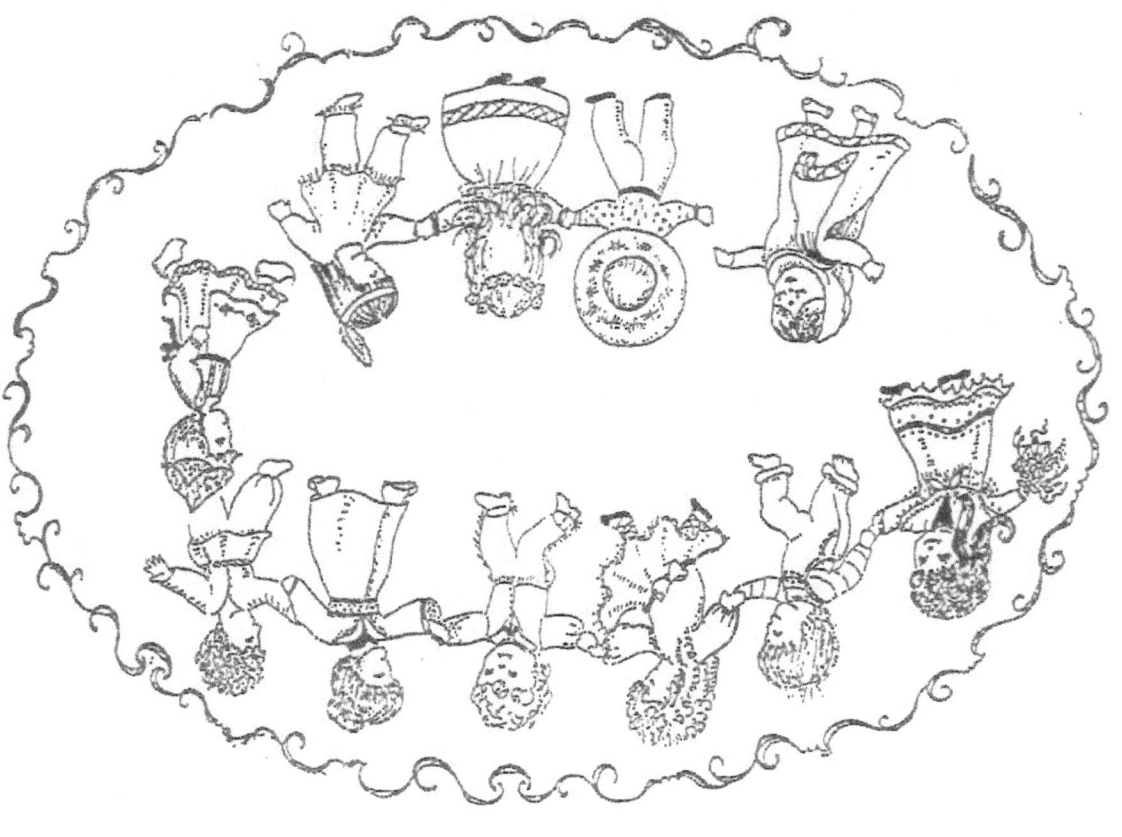

This card has been designed

with care and love especially

for you. It is suitable for framing.

Original drawing by

Louise Jackson, M.D.A.

Artistically colored by

_____

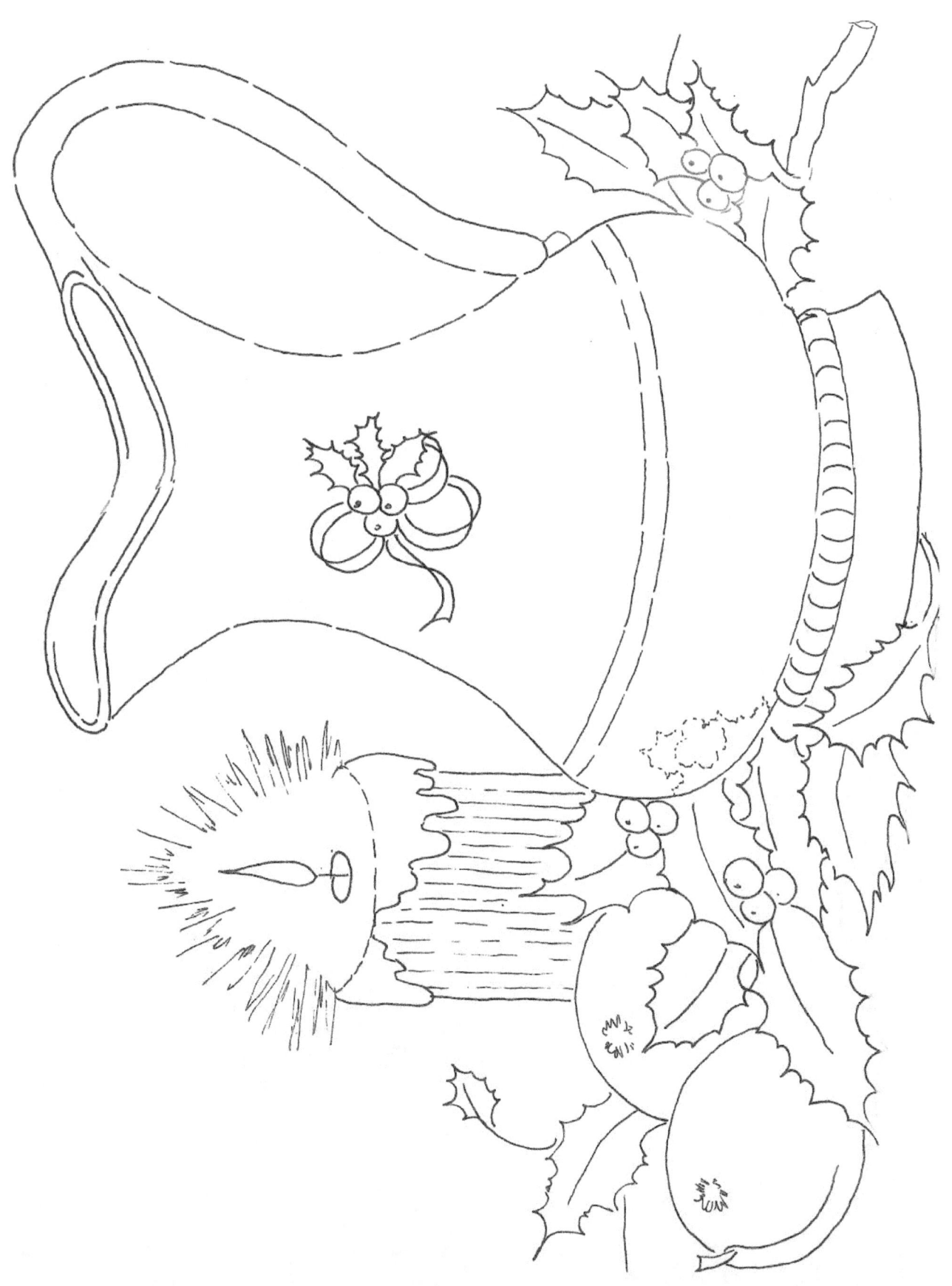

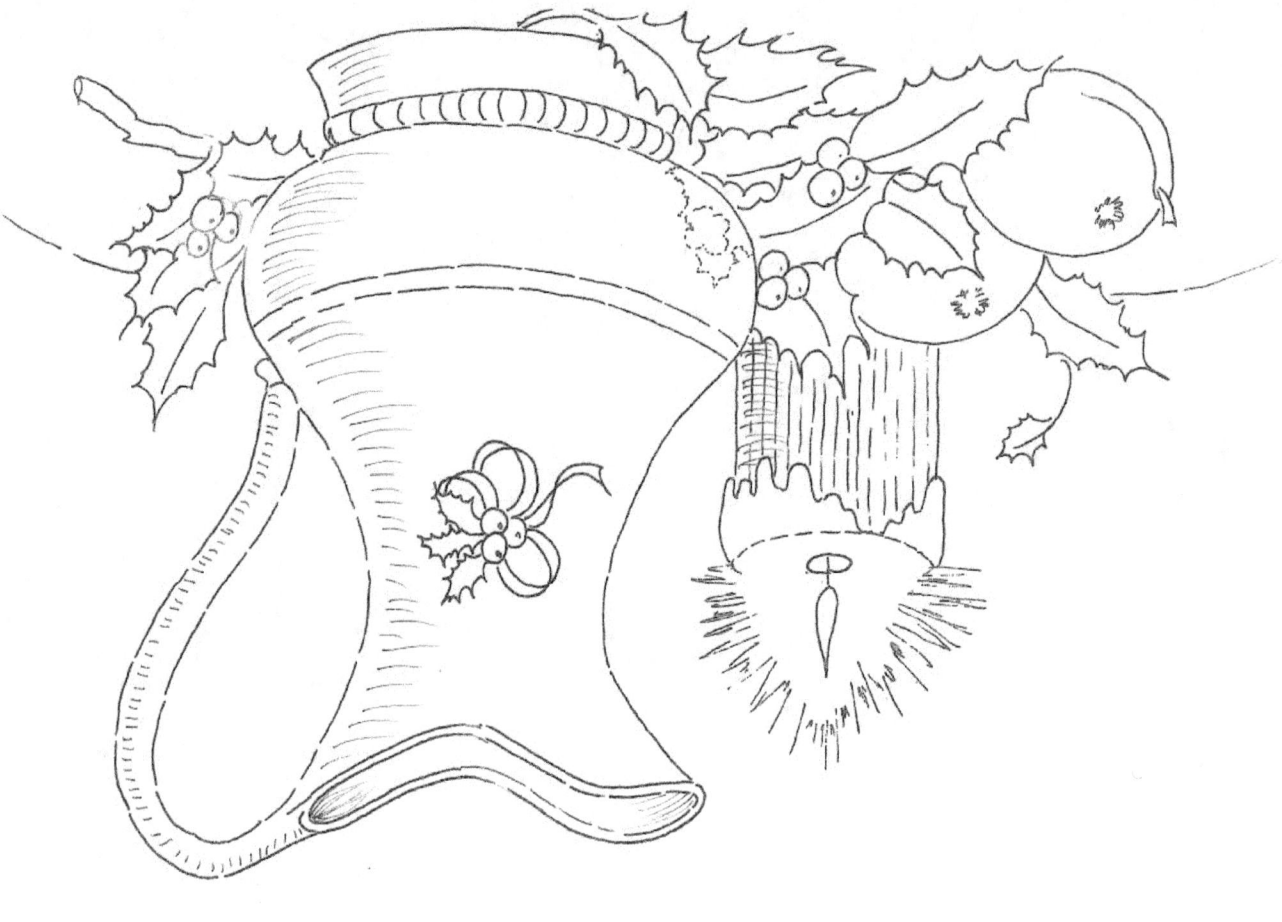

This card has been designed

with care and love especially

for you. It is suitable for framing.

Original drawing by

Louise Jackson, M.D.A.

Artistically colored by

_____

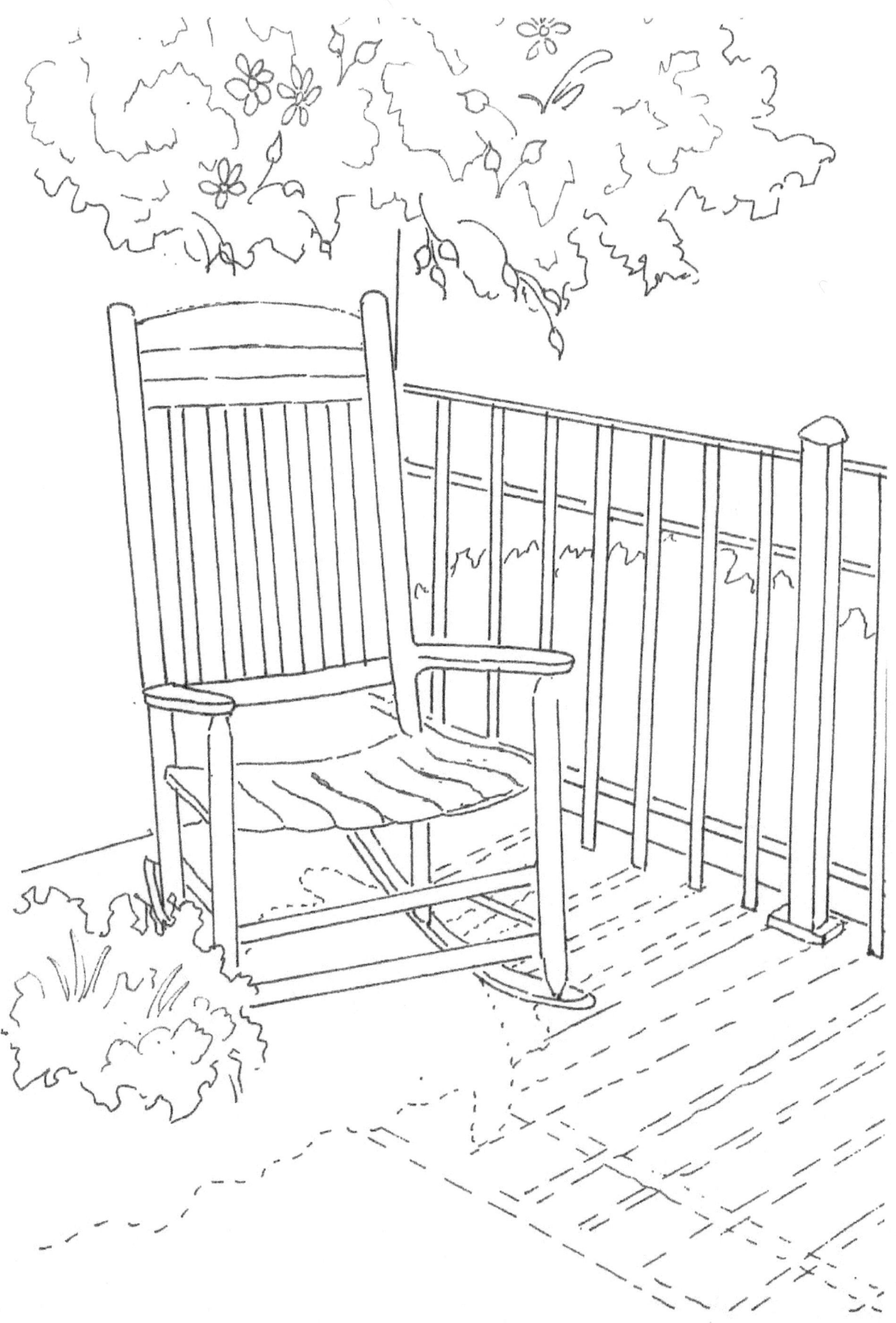

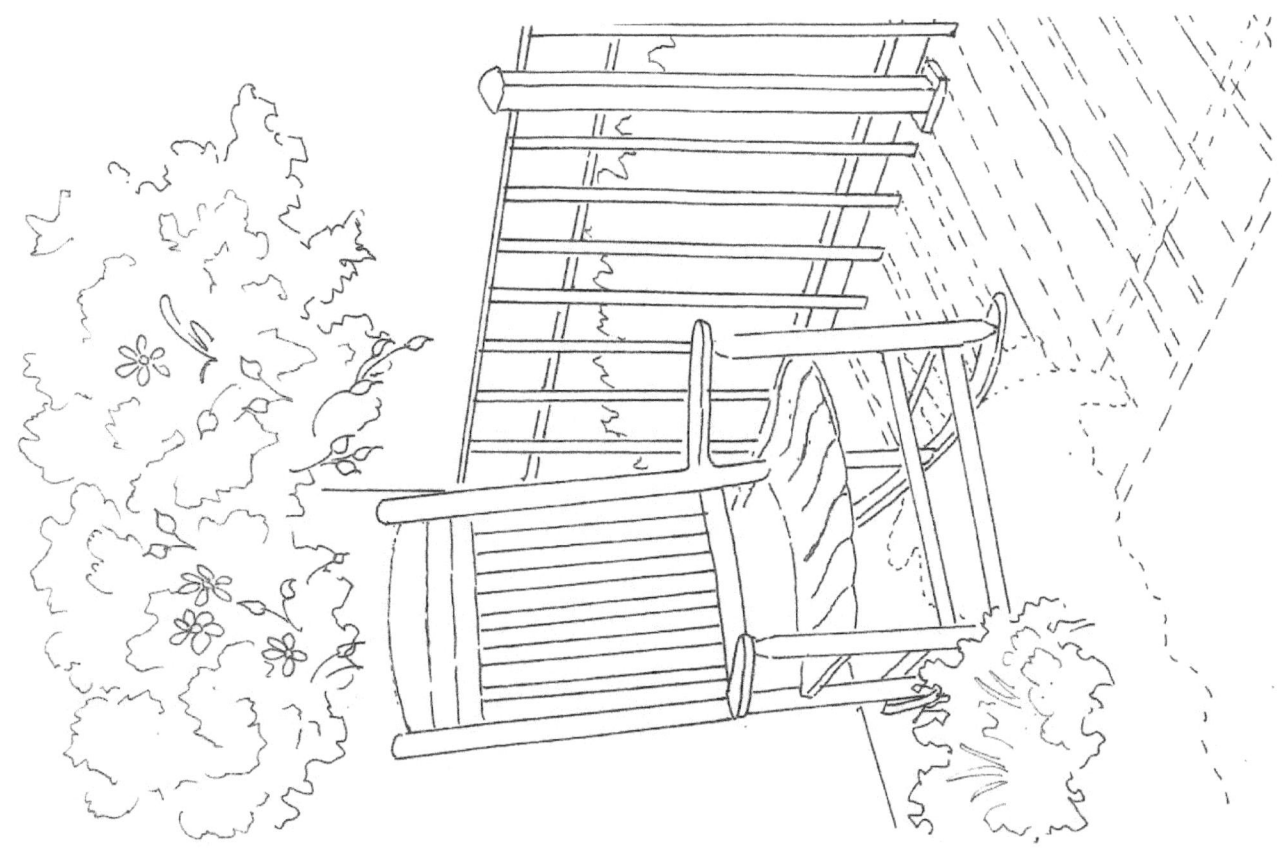

This card has been designed

with care and love especially

for you. It is suitable for framing.

Original drawing by

Louise Jackson, M.D.A.

Artistically colored by

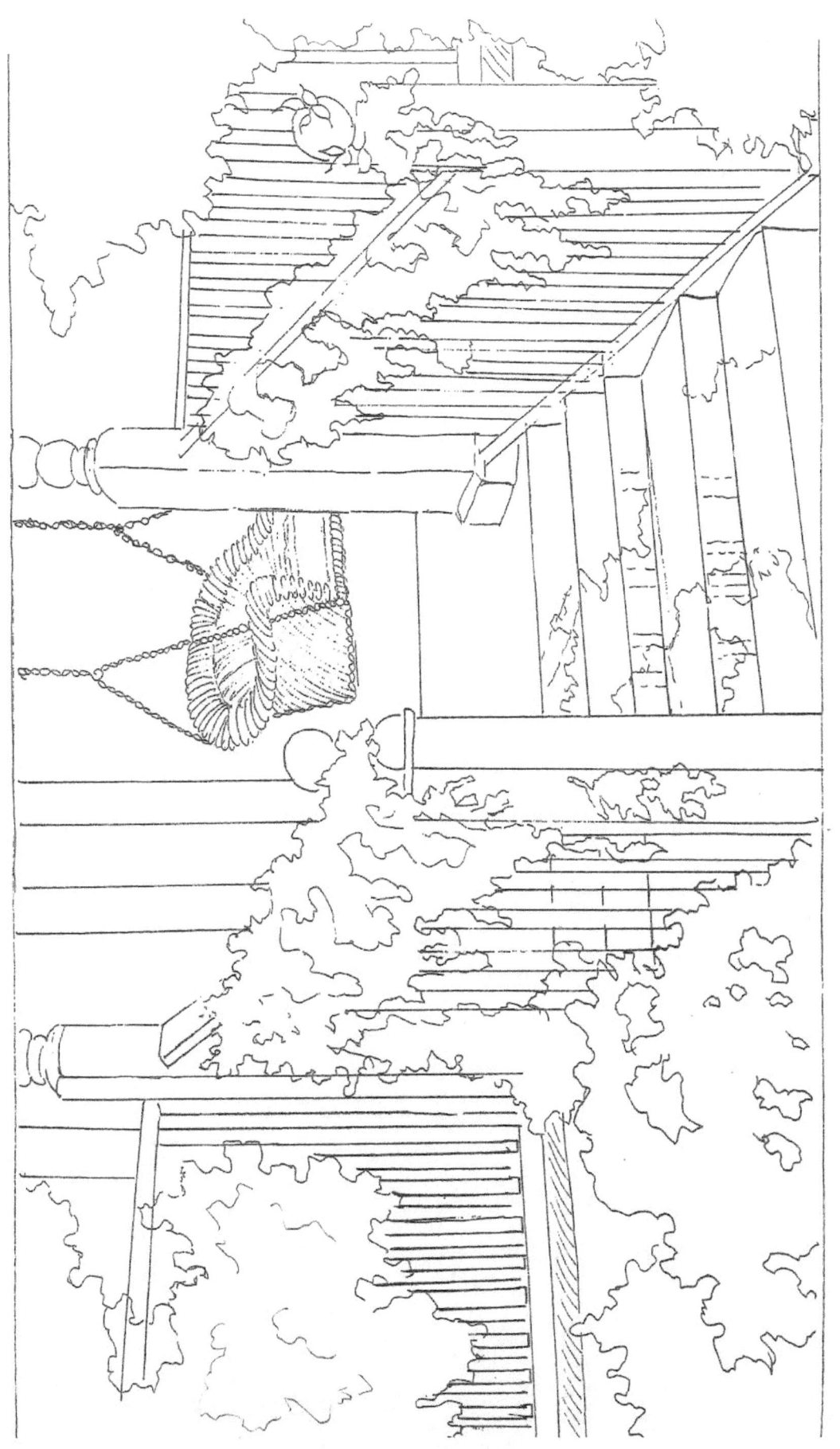

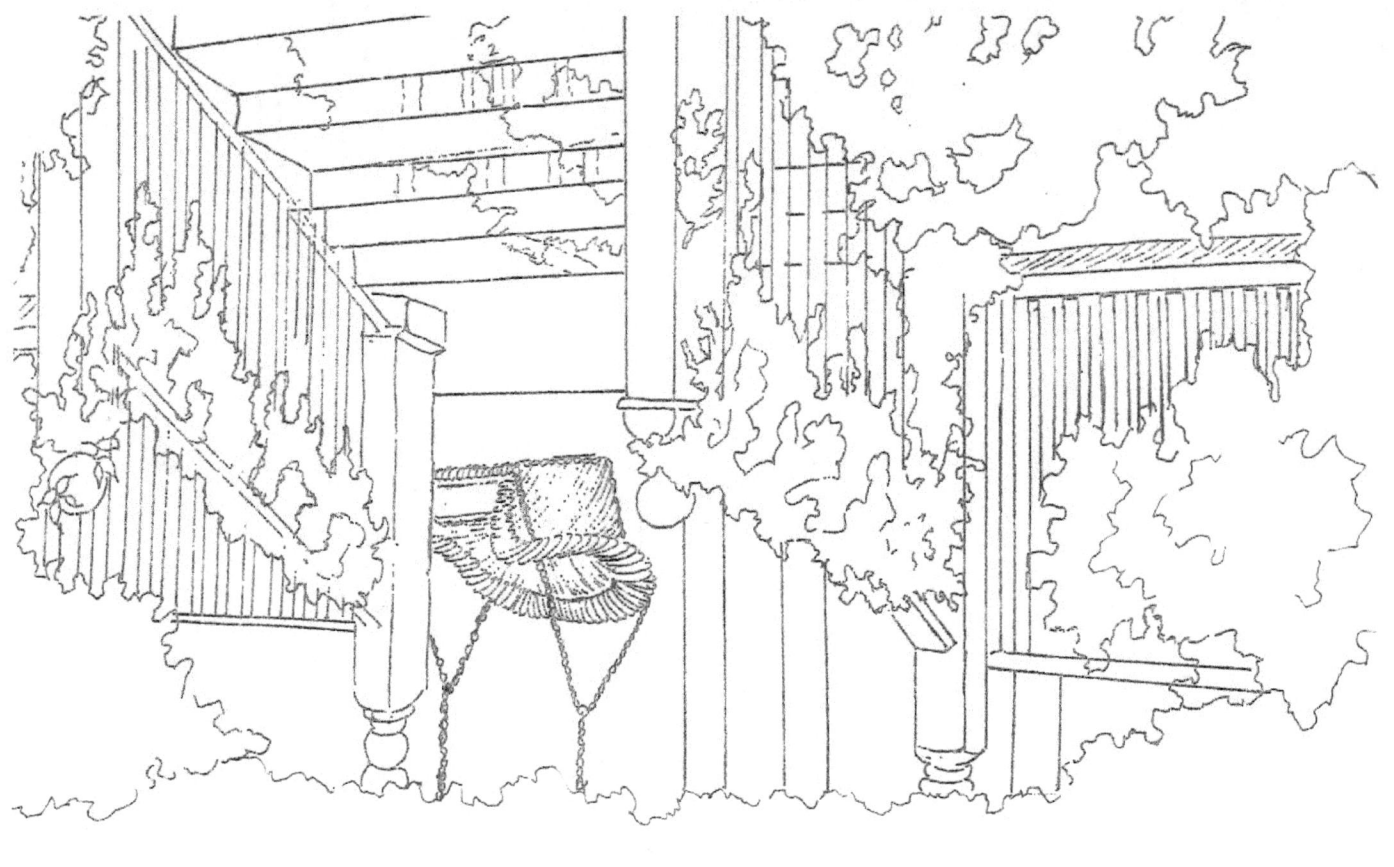

This card has been designed

with care and love especially

for you. It is suitable for framing.

Original drawing by

Louise Jackson, M.D.A.

Artistically colored by

_____

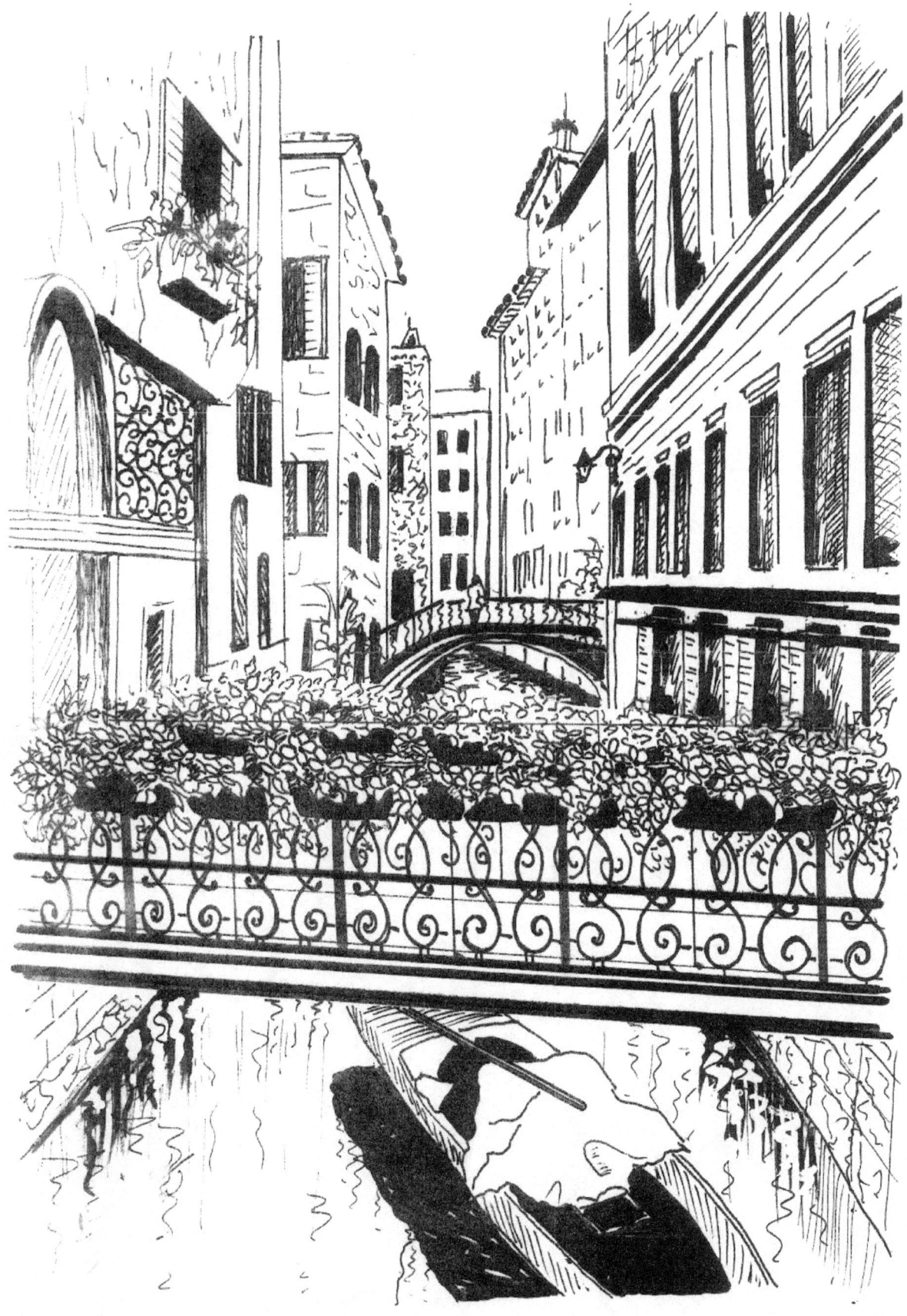

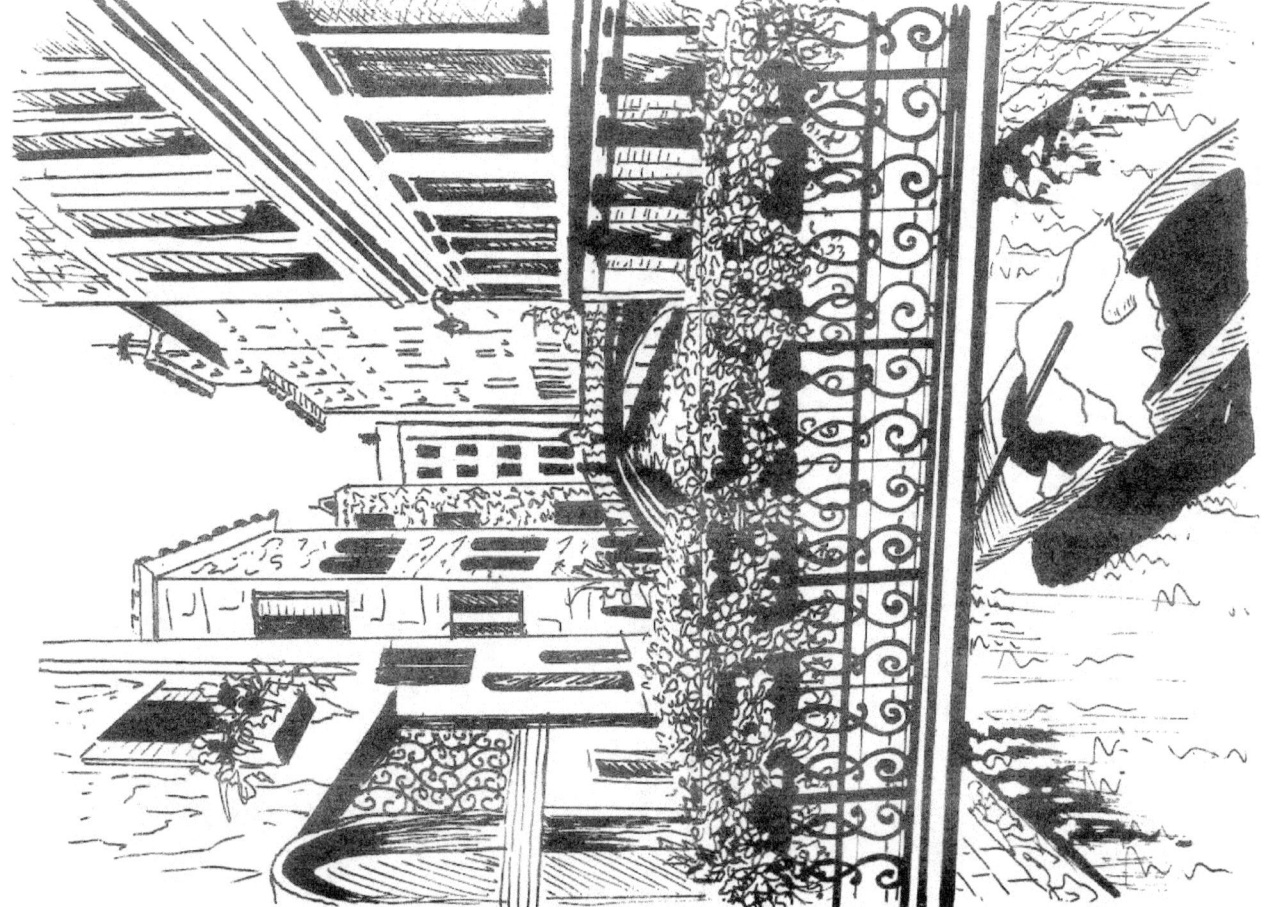

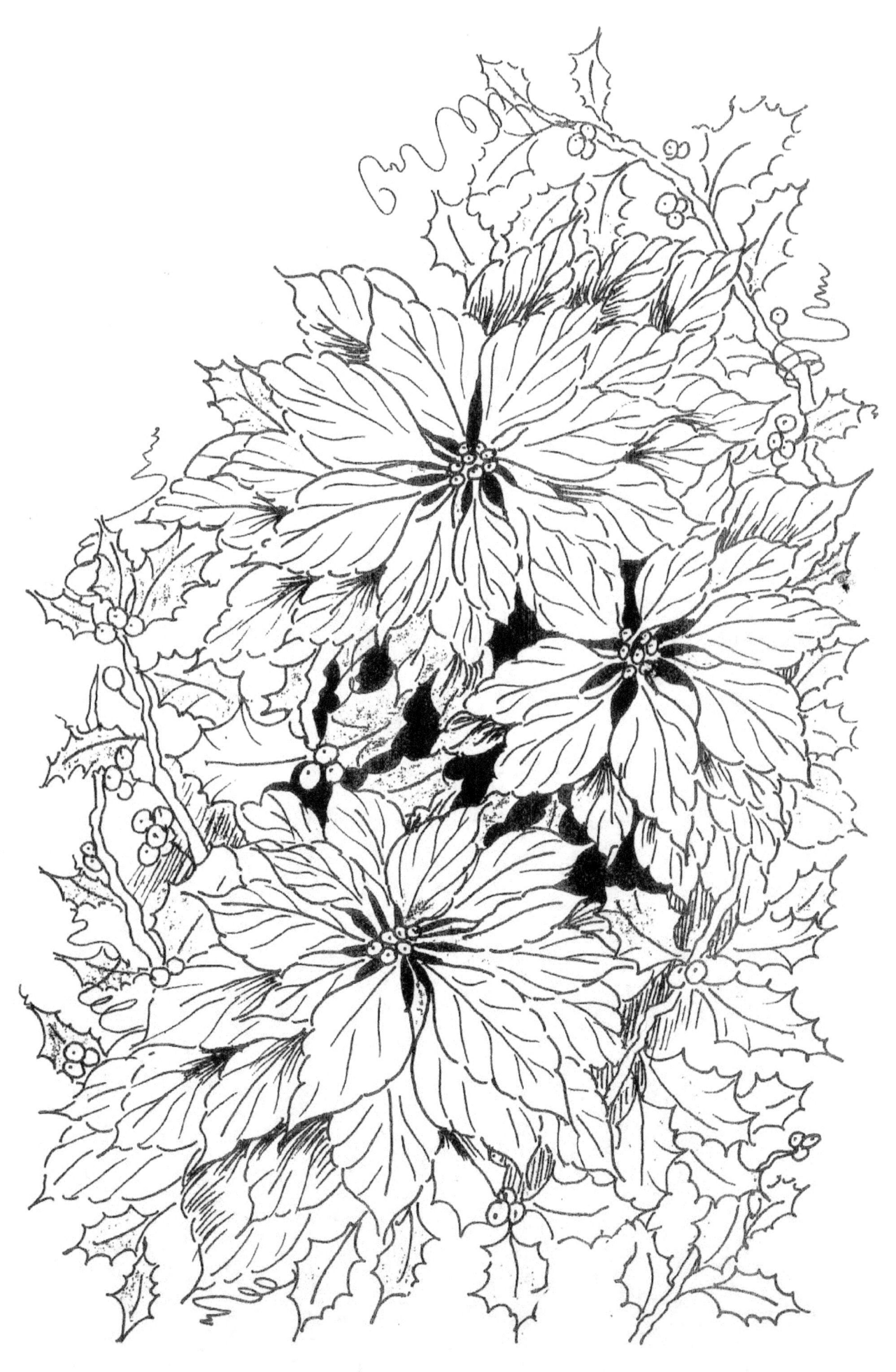

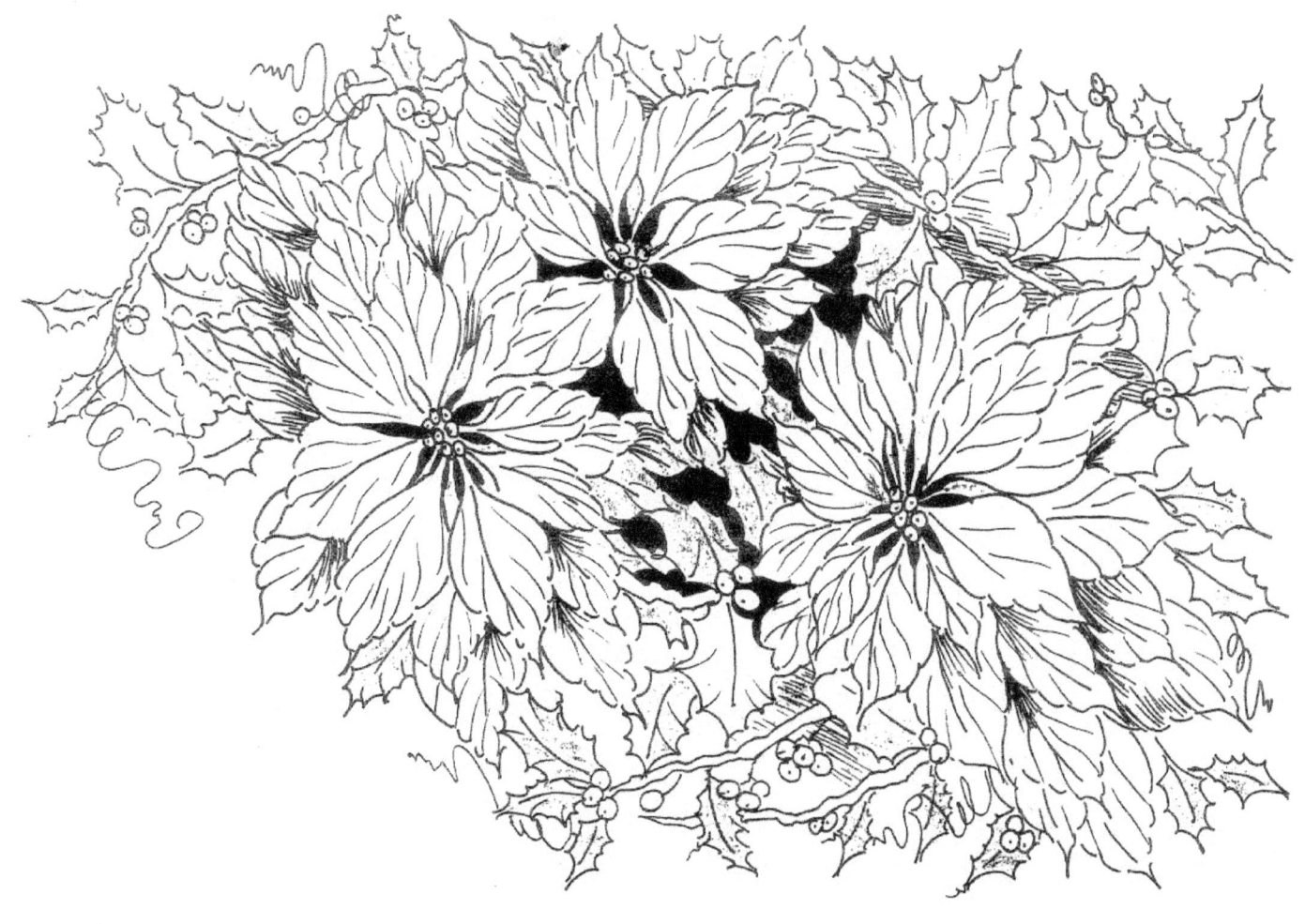

This little card has been
designed and painted with
care and love, especially
for you. It is suitable
for framing.

Original drawing by
Louise Jackson M.D.A.

Hand Painted by:

_____

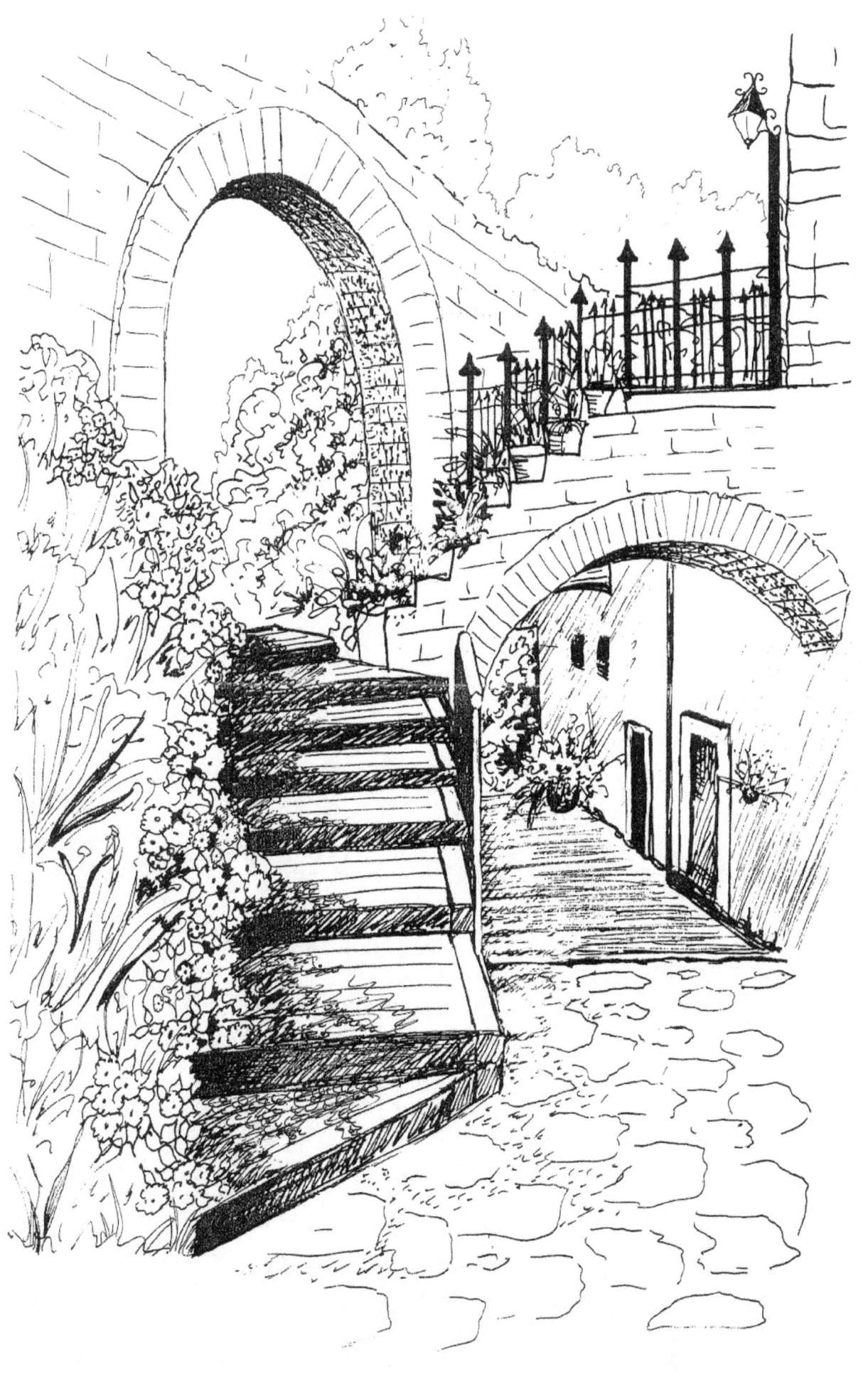

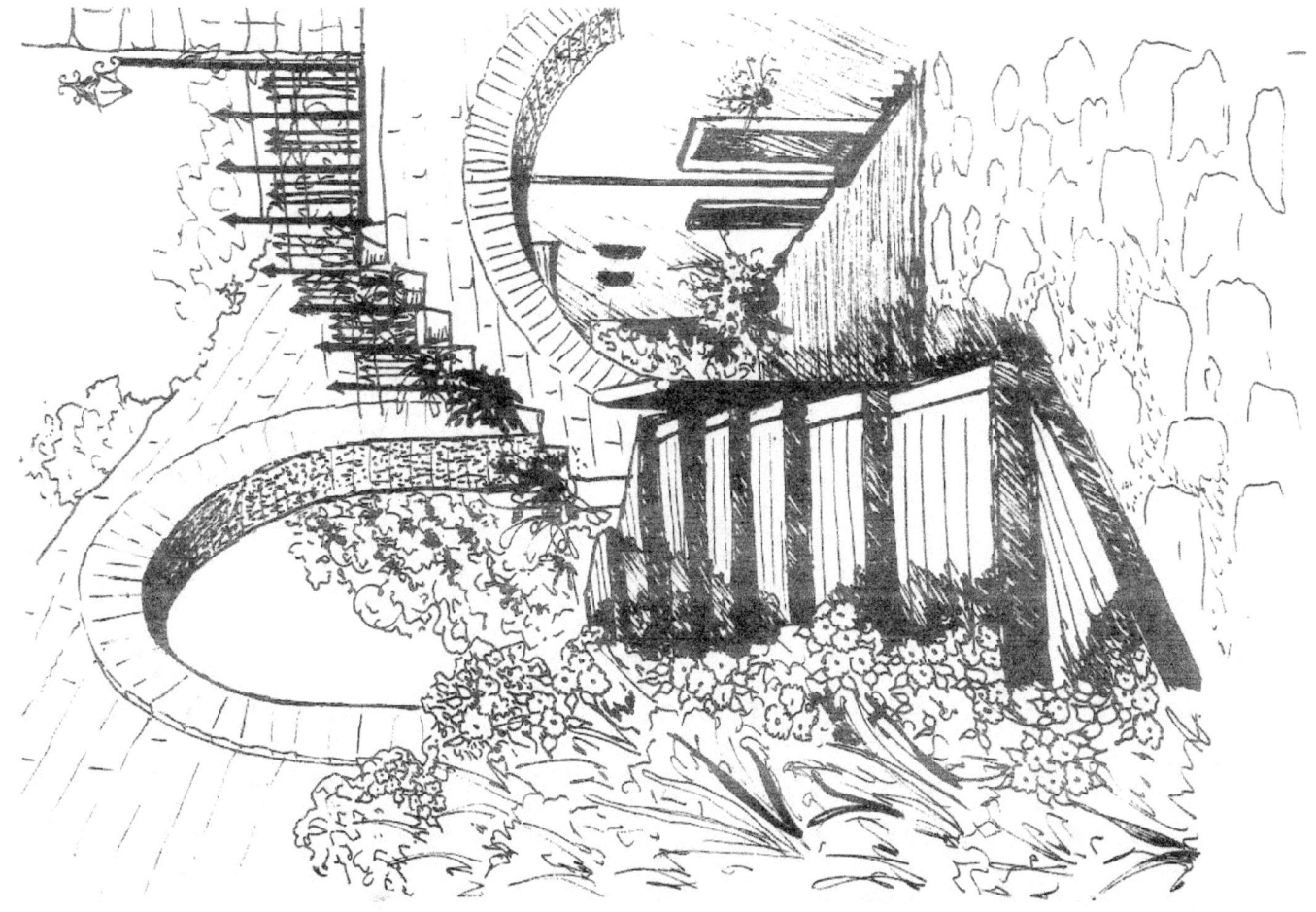

This card has been designed
and painted with care and love,
especially for you. It is suitable
for framing.

Original drawing by
Louise Jackson M.D.A.
"Italy Series"
Hand Painted by:

_____